Whispers of Christmas

A Tale of Joy and Wonder

Introduction

Christmas has always been a time of magic, where the world seems to slow down, and the air fills with a sense of anticipation. It's a season that invites wonder, reflection, and the rekindling of old traditions. But beyond the glittering lights, the sound of carolers, and the delicious scent of festive treats, there is something deeper—something timeless—that draws us together. Whispers of Christmas: A Tale of Joy and Wonder seeks to explore the true heart of the Christmas season.

This book is more than just a collection of holiday stories. It is an invitation to rediscover the simple joys of Christmas, the ones that come not from material gifts but from the connections we share with others. It's a celebration of family, kindness, and the joy of giving. Through each chapter, we will take a journey into the very essence of what makes Christmas so special—the magic of shared moments, the warmth of traditions, and the lasting impact of love and compassion.

In these pages, we will meet characters who, just like us, are swept up in the hustle and bustle of the season. They are faced with challenges, yet find themselves touched by the grace and wonder that Christmas brings. We will follow their journeys through snow-covered streets, joyful gatherings, and quiet, reflective moments as they learn that the true gifts of Christmas lie not in what we receive but in what we give—both to others and to ourselves.

As you read Whispers of Christmas, you will feel the magic of the season come alive. You will find yourself remembering the warmth of a family gathering, the quiet beauty of a snow-covered morning, and the unspoken joy of sharing a meal with those you love.

Whether you are curled up by the fire or sharing stories with friends, these tales will remind you of the wonder that Christmas brings to all of us.

Christmas is a time of joy, but it's also a time of deep reflection, of remembering the things that matter most, and of looking forward with hope. In a world that often feels rushed and chaotic, this book invites you to slow down, embrace the quiet moments, and let the whispers of Christmas fill your heart with peace, joy, and wonder.

May these pages inspire you to create new traditions, to deepen your connections with others, and to find joy in the little things that make the Christmas season so extraordinary. Welcome to Whispers of Christmas: A Tale of Joy and Wonder—where every story is a reminder that the true spirit of Christmas lies not in the gifts we give, but in the love we share.

Chapter 1

The Magic of the Season

The first snowfall of the season always carries a sense of enchantment, as if the world has been transformed into a wonderland overnight. The crisp air is filled with the scent of pine, and the streets sparkle under a blanket of snow, creating a scene so serene and perfect that it almost feels like a dream. The magic of Christmas is woven into every snowflake that falls, every twinkling light that adorns the trees, and every breath of cold air that reminds us of the season's arrival. As the days shorten and the chill of winter settles in, the anticipation for what's to come builds with each passing moment, igniting the spirit of the holidays in every heart.

There is something undeniably magical about the way Christmas brings people together, uniting them in ways both big and small. It's a time when families gather, when traditions are passed down, and when the world seems to pause for a moment, allowing us to reconnect with the joy of the season. The holiday season offers a respite from the rush of everyday life, encouraging us to slow down and savor the moments. Whether it's the simple act of decorating a tree or the thrill of preparing a home for visitors, these small rituals become part of the Christmas magic, creating lasting memories that warm the soul.

Yet, the magic of the season isn't just about the visible sights and sounds—it's about the quiet moments that often go unnoticed. It's the feeling of peace that washes over us as we sit by a crackling fire, the smile exchanged with a stranger in the midst of holiday shopping, or the joy found in the act of giving. The magic of the season is found in these shared experiences, where wonder and gratitude fill the air. In this chapter, we'll explore how Christmas, through its traditions, sights, and sounds, has the power to awaken the childlike sense of wonder within us all, reminding us that the true magic of the season is found in the love and joy we bring to one another.

The First Snowfall

There's something profoundly magical about the first snowfall of the season. It's a moment that stands apart, an event that stirs the soul and fills the air with a sense of wonder. The world seems to hold its breath, awaiting the soft descent of tiny crystals that will transform the ordinary into something extraordinary. It's not just the sight of snow that captivates us; it's the promise of a new beginning, a fresh start, and a world momentarily suspended in stillness and beauty.

As the first flakes begin to fall from the sky, there's a quiet anticipation that spreads through the air. The cold breeze carries a sharpness, almost electric, as if it knows that something incredible is about to happen. The landscape slowly transforms before our eyes: trees that were once barren now seem to wear their white coats like proud sentinels, standing tall against the gray sky. Each snowflake, delicate and unique, floats to the ground, adding to the growing blanket of white that softens the edges of everything it touches. Streets, homes, and rooftops, once defined by their hard, sharp lines, now appear smoothed and softened, enveloped in a gentle quiet.

The beauty of the first snowfall is often its fleeting nature—this moment, where everything is untouched and pristine, will soon be altered by the passage of time. The snow may accumulate in the corners of the streets, creating drifts, and people will begin to make their footprints, leaving traces of their passage in the newly-formed white world. But before that happens, there's an unparalleled serenity, a brief period of perfect stillness. The crunch of boots on fresh snow, the sound of wind brushing through the frosty air, and the laughter of children as they rush outside to catch snowflakes on their tongues all add to the magic of the moment.

For many, the first snowfall is a signal that the holiday season has arrived. It's as if the earth itself is preparing for the celebrations ahead, cloaking the world in a blanket of purity and peace. The sight of snow-covered trees and rooftops seems to stir memories of Christmases past—of cozy nights by the fire, of hot cocoa shared with family, and of the joy of unwrapping presents. The first snowfall triggers a flood of emotions, evoking nostalgia for simpler times, for a childlike innocence that still believes in the wonder of the season. The falling snow is a gentle reminder of the joy that comes from small moments of magic, where even the world's most ordinary sights can become extraordinary.

But the magic of the first snowfall extends beyond mere nostalgia. It's a tangible reminder of the beauty that can emerge from the simplest of things. The way the snowflakes glisten in the dim light of early morning, the way they seem to dance in the air before settling, are all part of a larger story—one that speaks to the beauty and wonder of nature, of life, and of the season itself. Snow reminds us to pause, to notice the quiet miracles unfolding around us, and to embrace the stillness that allows for reflection, joy, and peace.

In the moments after the first snowfall, the world feels renewed, as if the earth has been given a fresh canvas. The magic lies not only in the snowflakes themselves but in what they represent: a chance to begin again, to embrace the season with open arms, and to rediscover the wonder that exists in the smallest details of life. And so, as we step out into the winter air, the first snowfall reminds us that magic is real and that the world, in all its beauty, is a gift waiting to be experienced anew with every season.

Preparations for the Holiday

The preparations for the holiday season are a special kind of magic, a blend of excitement, nostalgia, and anticipation. They start long before the first snowflake falls, taking root in the small, quiet moments of daily life. The air seems to shift as the calendar moves closer to Christmas, and with it comes a wave of activities that fill the days with purpose and joy. Whether it's the thrill of decorating the house or the rush of finding the perfect gift, these preparations set the stage for the warmth and togetherness that the holidays promise.

One of the first signs that the holiday season is near is the arrival of the decorations. The house, once simple and understated, begins to transform. From twinkling fairy lights strung across windows to wreaths adorned with pinecones and ribbons, each decoration adds a touch of festivity to the surroundings. The scent of pine and cinnamon fills the air as Christmas trees are selected, hauled home, and carefully placed in living rooms. The excitement that accompanies picking out a tree—whether it's a real one, full of character with its branches reaching outward in all directions, or an artificial tree that comes to life with an explosion of lights and ornaments—is palpable. There's something deeply sentimental about placing the first ornament on the tree, a tradition that has been passed down through generations, each decoration carrying its own story, and in turn, weaving a new chapter into the family's holiday narrative.

As the house begins to glow with the spirit of the season, the next task is often the preparation of the holiday meal. This is no small feat, especially for families who follow cherished recipes passed down through the years. Kitchens are filled with the sounds of chopping, stirring, and baking as cookies, pies, and roasts take shape. The scent of gingerbread cookies baking in the oven or the rich aroma of a Christmas ham roasting in the kitchen is enough to make anyone's heart swell with warmth. The holiday meal is more than just food—it's a symbol of togetherness and love. Each dish, carefully prepared, becomes a part of a larger ritual that binds family and friends together in a shared experience of joy, laughter, and connection. For some, the process of preparing the meal is a meditative act, a way to reflect on the meaning of the season while honoring the traditions that make it special.

Alongside the decorating and cooking, the excitement of gift-giving looms large. The quest for the perfect gift is an art form in itself—one that combines thoughtfulness, creativity, and sometimes a little bit of stress. The act of selecting a present for a loved one is personal, a reflection of one's knowledge of their tastes, wishes, and needs. Shopping trips to crowded malls or cozy boutiques, wrapped in the warmth of hot cocoa or a winter coat, become small adventures. But it's not just about the presents themselves; it's about the joy of giving. The wrapping of gifts—carefully chosen paper, bows, and ribbons—is as much a part of the experience as the moment the gift is opened. Each gift, no matter how big or small, carries a message of love, appreciation, and connection.

As the days leading up to Christmas pass, the preparations take on a rhythm of their own. The house becomes a canvas for the season's spirit, the kitchen a place of creation, and the heart a vessel of anticipation. There's a certain harmony in the hustle and bustle of preparing for the holiday. It's in the way families come together to decorate, the laughter that echoes through the kitchen as cookies are baked, and the warmth that fills the room as gifts are shared. In these preparations, we find not just the outward trappings of the season but the deeper significance of what Christmas is truly about—a time to celebrate the joy of being together, to embrace the beauty of tradition, and to look forward with hope and love to the days ahead.

A Glimpse of Wonder

The holiday season often feels like a time when the ordinary becomes extraordinary, where the world around us shifts, if only for a moment, into a realm of wonder. Amid the excitement, the lights, and the traditions, there are fleeting moments of magic that appear unexpectedly, often when we least expect them. These moments, small and quiet yet profound, offer a glimpse into the heart of what makes the Christmas season so special. They are the moments that remind us of the joy, the beauty, and the mystery that the holiday holds, if only we take the time to notice.

One of the most powerful glimpses of wonder during the holiday season happens when we witness the pure excitement of a child discovering the magic of Christmas. The first time they see the twinkling lights on the Christmas tree or hear the sound of carolers singing in the distance, their eyes widen with awe and delight. It's as if, for them, the world is brimming with possibility. They believe in the magic of Santa Claus, in the beauty of snowflakes, and in the wonder of Christmas morning. Watching their faces light up with joy reminds us of the innocence and excitement that come with the season, of the way Christmas holds a certain kind of enchantment that is often hard to find as we grow older. These moments are a reminder of the magic that is all around us, and how easy it is to lose sight of it unless we take a moment to stop and appreciate the wonder.

Yet, the glimpses of wonder aren't limited to children's joy. They also manifest in the quiet, often unnoticed moments that arise when we are fully present in the season. For example, stepping outside into a world covered in fresh snow, the way the world seems to pause for a moment as if it's holding its breath. The air is crisp and clean, and the silence is almost sacred, broken only by the soft crunch of footsteps in the snow. The streetlights reflect off the ice, casting long shadows and giving everything a magical glow. It's a moment that can be easily overlooked in the rush of holiday preparations, but when we stop and take it all in, it feels like the universe is gifting us a fleeting glimpse of perfection. In these moments, we realize that the true magic of Christmas is not found in extravagant gifts or festive parties but in the quiet beauty of the world around us and in the sense of peace that comes when we allow ourselves to embrace it.

There's also a sense of wonder to be found in the acts of kindness and generosity that surface during the holiday season. Christmas has a way of bringing out the best in people. Whether it's a stranger holding the door open for you as you juggle bags of gifts, a friend offering a helping hand with holiday preparations, or a family member giving a thoughtful, unexpected gift, these moments of kindness often take us by surprise. They remind us that, at its heart, Christmas is about more than just the material aspects of the season; it's about love, connection, and giving from the heart. When we witness these small gestures of goodwill, we get a glimpse of the deeper meaning of the holiday—a reminder that the greatest gifts are not wrapped in shiny paper but are found in the love and care we offer one another.

As we move through the hustle and bustle of the holiday season, it's easy to become overwhelmed by the demands of shopping, cooking, and entertaining. But if we allow ourselves to pause, even for a brief moment, we can catch these glimpses of wonder—whether in the laughter of loved ones gathered around the table, the stillness of a snowy night, or the warm embrace of someone we hold dear. These moments, fleeting as they may be, are what make the holiday season so magical. They remind us that Christmas is not just about the grand celebrations or the perfect presents; it's about the everyday moments of beauty, kindness, and connection that fill our hearts with wonder.

Chapter 2
The Spirit of Givin

As the holiday season unfolds, there is one central theme that stands out above all others: the spirit of giving. Christmas has always been a time for selfless acts, where people come together to share their love, kindness, and generosity. It's a season that encourages us to look beyond ourselves and extend a hand to those in need. The act of giving, whether it's through material gifts, acts of service, or simply offering our time and attention, brings a unique sense of fulfillment and joy. In a world that often feels rushed and focused on individual pursuits, Christmas reminds us that true happiness is found in the act of giving, in offering something meaningful to others.

The beauty of the spirit of giving lies in its simplicity. It's not about the size or cost of the gift; rather, it's about the thought, care, and love that go into it. The greatest gifts are often those that come from the heart. A homemade card, a thoughtful gesture, or a kind word can mean just as much as the most expensive presents. During Christmas, we are reminded that the true value of a gift lies not in its price tag, but in the love and intention behind it. This chapter will explore how the spirit of giving transcends the material and brings people closer, fostering connections that are deeper and more lasting than any physical object could ever achieve.

At its core, the spirit of giving is about creating a sense of community and belonging. Christmas offers an opportunity to reach out to those we may not see regularly—friends, family, neighbors, and even strangers. Whether it's through donating to charity, offering a helping hand, or simply taking the time to listen to someone, these small acts of kindness have the power to transform lives. In this chapter, we will explore how the simple act of giving, no matter how big or small, has the ability to create ripples of joy and warmth that extend far beyond the holiday season. It's through giving that we experience the true meaning of Christmas, finding fulfillment not in what we receive, but in what we offer to others.

Acts of Kindness

During the Christmas season, acts of kindness take on a special significance. While we may strive to be kind year-round, it's during this time that the spirit of generosity truly shines. The holiday season is a reminder of the power of small, thoughtful gestures that can make a world of difference in someone's life. Whether it's a simple smile or a grand gesture of support, kindness creates an atmosphere of warmth and connection that transforms the way we experience the world. It's a gift that costs nothing but can leave a lasting impact, not just on the person receiving it, but on the giver as well.

One of the most profound acts of kindness is the act of giving without expectation. Often, the holiday season becomes a time when we are encouraged to think beyond our own needs and desires. It's a time to reflect on the blessings we have and to share them with others. A small donation to a local charity, a thoughtful gift for a friend, or volunteering at a soup kitchen can make a tangible difference in someone's life. What makes these acts powerful is not just the material gift or support itself but the intention behind it. The true spirit of kindness lies in offering help without seeking anything in return, in giving because we genuinely care about others and want to see them happy and comfortable, especially during this time of year.

Acts of kindness are not always grand, and often, it's the smaller, more personal gestures that have the most profound impact. For example, checking in on a neighbor who might be lonely, offering a ride to someone in need, or simply sending a heartfelt note to a friend can brighten their day in unexpected ways. These actions may seem simple, but they communicate something powerful: that someone is thinking of them, that they matter, and that they are not alone. In a time when many people struggle with isolation or hardship, even the smallest act of kindness can feel like a lifeline. It's in these moments that we truly understand the power of human connection, the bond that forms when we extend ourselves to others.

What's beautiful about kindness is that it's contagious. When we act with kindness, we often inspire others to do the same. The ripple effect of a simple gesture of goodwill can extend far beyond what we initially see. A single act of kindness can inspire a chain reaction, creating a wave of positivity and compassion that spreads throughout a community. One person's willingness to give, whether in the form of time, attention, or resources, encourages others to do the same, fostering a sense of unity and shared purpose. This season, as we give to others, we are also creating an environment where kindness thrives, where the world feels just a little bit warmer and more hopeful.

In this chapter, we explore how the simple but profound act of kindness can be a defining feature of the Christmas season. It's in the little things—the smile exchanged with a stranger, the help offered to a friend, the moment of connection shared with someone in need—that we find the true magic of the holiday. It's a reminder that the holiday season is not just about the big events or the extravagant celebrations, but about the quiet, everyday moments where we show up for each other, where kindness becomes the most meaningful gift of all. In a world that sometimes feels divided, these acts of kindness have the power to heal, to unite, and to make us all feel, even for a brief moment, that the world is a little bit better.

Gifts from the Heart

There's a unique kind of magic that comes with giving a gift that is born from the heart. Unlike gifts that are chosen for their price or popularity, these are the gifts that reflect a deep connection between the giver and the receiver. They carry meaning, thoughtfulness, and care—qualities that go far beyond the material value of the item. These are the gifts that speak to the soul, that convey love, appreciation, and a recognition of the person's worth. When a gift comes from the heart, it becomes far more than an object; it becomes a symbol of affection, thoughtfulness, and emotional connection.

At the heart of these gifts is the idea of personalization. A gift from the heart doesn't have to be extravagant or expensive; it just needs to be meaningful. Perhaps it's a handmade item, something crafted with care and skill, or a gesture that requires time and effort rather than money. Maybe it's a framed photo of a cherished memory, a hand-written letter that captures the emotions and thoughts that words often fail to express, or even a song written for someone special. The value of these gifts doesn't lie in their cost, but in their emotional significance. They reflect the time and energy the giver has invested, the understanding they have of the recipient's interests, and the bond they share.

There is a certain vulnerability in giving a gift from the heart, as it reveals a piece of the giver's spirit. When we choose to give from the heart, we're offering not just an item, but a part of ourselves. It's an expression of how much we care, how well we know someone, and how much we value their place in our lives. These gifts don't need to be perfect or flawless—they simply need to show that they were given with love and thought. Whether it's a carefully chosen book for an avid reader, a knitted scarf made with patience and care, or a shared experience, the gift becomes a reflection of the relationship, a moment of shared meaning between two people.

Furthermore, gifts from the heart have a unique power to create lasting memories. A gift like this carries with it not just the moment of giving, but the warmth and joy that come with it. Years later, the recipient may not remember the exact item, but they will recall the emotion behind it, the thoughtfulness and care that went into it. It becomes part of the story of the relationship—the moments spent together, the bond that deepens with each thoughtful gesture. These gifts have the power to remind people that they are loved, valued, and cherished, not just for what they have, but for who they are.

The beauty of gifts from the heart lies in their ability to transcend the material world and touch the deeper aspects of human connection. While holiday shopping can sometimes feel like a checklist, a gift from the heart breaks free from this transactional nature. It's not about finding the perfect item from a store or following the latest trend—it's about creating a moment of genuine connection, a moment where the recipient feels seen and understood. And in that simple act, a gift from the heart becomes a celebration of love, of the shared experiences that bind us together, and of the joy that comes from giving freely and sincerely.

As we give these gifts this holiday season, we are reminded that it is not the value of the gift that matters, but the sentiment behind it. Whether large or small, a gift from the heart becomes a lasting treasure, a tangible reminder of the intangible things that truly matter—love, kindness, and the unspoken bonds that connect us all.

The Joy of Sharing

At the heart of the holiday season, one of the most profound experiences we can have is the joy of sharing. While Christmas is often a time of receiving, it is the act of giving and sharing that fills our hearts with warmth and fulfillment. There is something deeply transformative about sharing, whether it's material gifts, experiences, or even our time and attention. The simple act of sharing—of opening our hearts and lives to others—creates bonds that transcend the physical realm, enriching both the giver and the receiver in ways that money cannot buy.

The joy of sharing is rooted in the idea that when we give, we create a space for connection. It is an act that transcends the individual and extends to the community, the family, or even a complete stranger. This connection is especially evident during the holiday season, when people come together to celebrate and to share their blessings with those around them. Whether it's inviting friends or family to join in a holiday meal, sharing a heartfelt story, or offering a helping hand to someone in need, sharing fosters a sense of unity that brings people closer. There's a kind of magic in the simple act of gathering and sharing that elevates the moment, turning it into something special and memorable.

One of the most beautiful aspects of sharing is that it requires no grand gestures. In fact, some of the most meaningful acts of sharing are the simplest. It might be as small as offering a seat to someone who's standing, sharing your favorite homemade cookies with a neighbor, or lending a sympathetic ear to someone going through a difficult time. These small, thoughtful gestures of kindness often mean the most because they reflect genuine care and concern for others. The joy of sharing is not about the value of the object or the extent of the action; it's about the intention behind it. Every time we share something with someone else, whether it's a possession, an experience, or a piece of our time, we are telling that person, "You matter. You are worth my attention. I am happy to offer this to you."

The act of sharing also brings a deep sense of fulfillment. When we share, we experience the joy of making someone else happy, but we also gain something intangible in return. There is a profound sense of satisfaction that comes from knowing that we have made a positive impact in someone's life, even in the smallest of ways. It can be a smile, a thank-you, or the simple feeling of knowing that we've brightened someone's day. This sense of fulfillment is what often makes sharing so rewarding—it's not about the recognition or acknowledgment, but the inner satisfaction of knowing that we have made a difference. In this way, the joy of sharing is its own reward.

During Christmas, the joy of sharing often extends beyond just our immediate circle to those in need. The season encourages us to think of others who may not have the same privileges or comforts we do. Whether it's through donating to charity, volunteering at a local shelter, or simply offering support to someone going through a tough time, sharing becomes an act of compassion. It reminds us of our shared humanity and the power we have to bring light into someone else's life. These acts of generosity become part of the greater holiday spirit, transforming Christmas from a personal celebration into a collective act of kindness and love.

In essence, the joy of sharing is about making the world a little brighter, a little warmer, and a little more connected. It is through sharing that we create community, strengthen relationships, and spread goodwill. As we give, whether in small or large ways, we find that the act itself enriches us, filling our hearts with gratitude, compassion, and joy. This holiday season, the true magic lies not in the gifts we receive but in the joy we experience when we share with others—an act that reflects the true spirit of Christmas and the beauty of the human connection.

Chapter 3

A Christmas Eve to Remember

Christmas Eve is a night steeped in tradition and anticipation, a time when the magic of the holiday season comes alive in the hearts of those who gather to celebrate. As the world outside falls into a peaceful silence, there is an air of excitement that fills the homes, where families come together to honor the customs passed down through generations. The warmth of the evening contrasts with the cold winter night, and the flickering glow of candles and Christmas lights casts a soft, welcoming light across every room. For many, Christmas Eve holds a special place in the heart, a night when all the hustle and bustle of the season slows down, and the true meaning of Christmas begins to settle in.

For families, Christmas Eve is a time of shared rituals that carry with them a sense of continuity and comfort. From the excitement of preparing the holiday meal to the anticipation of gathering around the tree for the first time, the evening is filled with small, meaningful moments. Children eagerly hang their stockings by the fireplace, hoping for a glimpse of Santa's sleigh, while adults share laughter and stories, reminiscing about Christmases gone by. There's a joy in these traditions—both old and new—that creates a sense of belonging and togetherness. In this chapter, we will explore how these traditions help us reconnect with our roots, ground us in the present, and prepare us for the joyous celebration to come.

Yet, amidst the laughter and the festivities, Christmas Eve also has a deeper, quieter magic. It's a night that invites reflection and gratitude, a time to pause and appreciate the blessings of the past year. As families come together and friends share in the joy of the season, there's a collective sense of peace that permeates the night. Whether it's the sound of a beloved carol being sung softly, the gentle rhythm of wrapping paper being torn open, or simply the comfort of being surrounded by loved ones, Christmas Eve holds the promise of love and connection. It's a night that reminds us of what truly matters—the bonds we share, the love we give, and the memories we create. In this chapter, we'll delve into the beauty of this cherished night, exploring the moments of wonder, joy, and reflection that make Christmas Eve a night to remember.

Family Traditions

Family traditions hold a special place in the heart of every holiday season, particularly at Christmas. They are the threads that weave generations together, creating a sense of continuity and connection. These traditions, passed down from parents to children, create a bond that transcends time and distance, reminding us of our roots and the values that shape our families. From the first gingerbread cookie baked together to the lighting of the Christmas tree, family traditions are more than just customs; they are the very essence of the holiday, creating lasting memories that are cherished for years to come.

At the heart of every family tradition is the joy of shared experiences. Whether it's decorating the tree, preparing a special meal, or gathering around the fireplace to exchange gifts, these moments create a sense of togetherness that goes beyond the gifts and the decorations. It's about creating memories with the people we love, building a shared history that can be passed down to future generations. For many families, the act of decorating the Christmas tree is one of the most treasured traditions. The process is often a family affair, with each person contributing to the decoration, adding their own touch to the tree. The excitement of unwrapping ornaments, many of which are family heirlooms with stories of their own, fills the room with laughter and nostalgia. As the tree lights twinkle in the darkness, the sense of accomplishment and togetherness is palpable, reminding everyone that the holidays are not just about what's under the tree but about the moments shared in its creation.

Another cherished family tradition is the preparation of the holiday meal. For many, the act of cooking together is as important as the meal itself. Recipes that have been passed down for generations are lovingly prepared, with each family member playing a part in the process. From stirring the gravy to setting the table, every task is an opportunity to bond and create something together. The kitchen becomes a place of warmth, not only in temperature but in spirit. The smell of roasting meats, freshly baked bread, and spiced desserts fills the home, adding to the sense of anticipation and excitement. These meals are not just about nourishing the body but also about nourishing the soul, reinforcing the idea that food, like love, is best when shared.

Family traditions often extend beyond the confines of the home and into the community. For some, attending a Christmas Eve service or volunteering at a local charity becomes an important part of the holiday season. These acts of kindness not only reinforce the values of generosity and compassion but also create a sense of belonging within the larger community. By participating in these traditions, families instill in their children the importance of giving back and sharing with others, teaching them that Christmas is not just about receiving but about offering love and support to those in need.

What makes family traditions truly special is their ability to evolve while still maintaining a sense of familiarity and comfort. As children grow and new members join the family, these traditions adapt, creating new memories and experiences. New customs may be introduced, like a family movie night or a secret Santa exchange, but the core values that these traditions represent—love, connection, and gratitude—remain the same. It's the familiarity of these traditions, the knowledge that no matter where life may take us, we can always return to these moments of shared joy and celebration, that makes them so powerful.

Family traditions are a testament to the bonds that hold us together. They remind us that Christmas is not just about what we have or what we receive, but about the relationships that define our lives. These traditions, with all their joy, laughter, and love, create a sense of home that is both timeless and enduring. As each year passes, we find ourselves looking forward to the familiar rituals of the season, knowing that the love and warmth of our family traditions will always be there, waiting to welcome us home.

Unexpected Guests

There is a certain charm to the idea of unexpected guests arriving during the holiday season. While Christmas is often planned down to the smallest detail, it is in these unanticipated visits that the true magic of the season can unfold. The surprise of a knock on the door or the sound of carolers unexpectedly filling the air often becomes a moment to remember, a reminder that the spirit of Christmas is not just about the people we expect to gather around the table, but also about the surprises and unplanned moments that bring us closer to one another.

The arrival of unexpected guests often creates a ripple of excitement and a sense of unpredictability in the otherwise meticulously planned holiday. It's a moment when the holiday's true meaning—of love, togetherness, and kindness—becomes apparent. These guests may not always be relatives or close friends, but rather neighbors, acquaintances, or even strangers who find themselves in need of some warmth, companionship, or cheer. The spirit of generosity takes center stage, as families and hosts quickly open their homes and hearts, offering food, drinks, and holiday cheer. Whether it's an old friend who's passing through town or someone new to the community, the warmth of a spontaneous invitation can turn a quiet evening into something extraordinary.

For many, unexpected guests have a way of reminding us of the core values of Christmas—love, generosity, and hospitality. The natural inclination to offer a place at the table, to share a meal, and to make someone feel welcome is a hallmark of the season. Even if it means rearranging plans or adding an extra plate to the table, the gesture of opening one's home to a guest in need creates an atmosphere of goodwill and connection. It's a reminder that the true joy of the season lies in the connections we make, both planned and unplanned, and the kindness we extend to others, even when it's least expected.

Unexpected guests also often lead to the creation of spontaneous memories, ones that can become cherished for years to come. A shared cup of mulled wine by the fire, stories told late into the night, or laughter echoing through the house as everyone gets to know one another—these moments add depth and richness to the holiday experience. They are the memories that will be retold in future gatherings, the stories that will be shared and remembered long after the guests have left. These impromptu moments can also bring a fresh perspective to the holiday, allowing everyone to pause and appreciate the beauty of the present, rather than getting caught up in the details or expectations of the season. The surprise of an unexpected guest often shifts the focus from the material aspects of Christmas to the emotional and spiritual ones—the connection, the generosity, and the love that bind us all.

Moreover, unexpected guests can remind us of the importance of community. Christmas is a time when families gather, but it is also a time when we reach out to the broader circle of people in our lives. Sometimes, the most meaningful experiences come not from those we expect to see, but from those who find their way into our homes by chance or necessity. Whether it's a friend who has nowhere else to go, a neighbor who doesn't want to spend the evening alone, or a stranger who is simply in need of kindness, the presence of unexpected guests reminds us that Christmas is not about exclusivity but about inclusivity, about opening our hearts and homes to all.

In the end, the arrival of unexpected guests is a gift in itself—a reminder that life is full of surprises, and that the holiday season is about embracing those moments with open arms. These unplanned visitors offer opportunities to connect, to share, and to create memories that go far beyond the expectations of the season. They highlight the true meaning of Christmas: that the love we give and the hospitality we extend can bring joy and warmth not only to our closest loved ones but to anyone in need of it.

A Night of Peace

Amid the hustle and bustle of the Christmas season, there is a special kind of peace that settles in on Christmas Eve. It is a night like no other, where the world seems to pause for just a moment, allowing us to take a deep breath and reflect on the true meaning of the holiday. The streets, which are often filled with the noise of holiday shopping and the rush of last-minute preparations, are quieter now. The air is crisp and still, with the soft glow of Christmas lights casting a warm, serene light across homes and streets. It's a night where the chaos of everyday life melts away, and we are left with a sense of calm, a sense of peace that seems to envelop everything around us.

This night of peace is reflected in the atmosphere inside the home as well. The lights on the Christmas tree twinkle gently in the corner, and the faint scent of pine and cinnamon fills the air. The fireplace crackles with warmth, offering both physical comfort and a soothing backdrop to the quiet of the evening. It is a time when families gather together, leaving behind the distractions and stresses of the outside world. Whether it's enjoying a festive meal, sharing stories, or simply sitting together in the quiet of the evening, there is an unspoken connection that is felt deeply. The world outside may be moving quickly, but within the walls of the home, time slows down, allowing for moments of reflection, gratitude, and peace.

One of the most profound elements of this night of peace is the opportunity it provides for reflection. As the year draws to a close, Christmas Eve offers a time to pause and think about the blessings and challenges of the past year. There is space to appreciate the simple joys—the laughter shared with family, the warmth of good friendships, and the love that surrounds us. It is also a time to honor those we've lost or those who may be far away, holding them in our hearts as we gather with those still present. The stillness of the night creates an opening for these quiet reflections, where the noise of the world gives way to the deeper emotions that connect us to the true spirit of Christmas. It is in these moments of peace that we can most clearly hear the whispers of love, hope, and gratitude.

For many, a night of peace is also about spiritual connection. Christmas Eve, being the night before Christmas, carries with it a sacredness that transcends the festivities and the presents. It is a time when people of faith gather to celebrate the birth of Christ, reflecting on the profound message of peace and goodwill that the season represents. For those who attend midnight services or light candles in quiet reverence, this time offers a deep sense of spiritual peace. It is a time to center ourselves, to remember the importance of love, compassion, and kindness, and to renew our commitment to living these values throughout the coming year.

In addition to the inner peace it brings, the night is also a time when families create their own traditions of calm and serenity. Some may take a walk through the snow-covered streets, enjoying the peaceful quiet that surrounds them. Others might read a favorite Christmas story aloud, or listen to soft carols that fill the room with warmth. These traditions, no matter how simple, help to anchor the night in a sense of tranquility. The outside world may continue to rush forward, but within the home, a sense of peace reigns—a peace that comes from togetherness, from tradition, and from a collective sense of gratitude for the present moment.

A night of peace on Christmas Eve is not only a reprieve from the frenzy of the season but also a reminder of what truly matters. It is a night to reconnect with those we love, to reflect on the past and the future, and to find solace in the quiet moments that define the holiday. This peaceful night serves as the perfect prelude to the joy and celebration of Christmas Day, grounding us in the deeper meaning of the season and preparing our hearts for the blessings to come. It is in this tranquility that we find the true spirit of Christmas, one of love, peace, and goodwill toward all.

Chapter 4
The Story Behind the Tree

The Christmas tree stands as the centerpiece of holiday celebrations, its sparkling lights and festive ornaments creating an atmosphere of joy and wonder. However, beyond the twinkling lights and colorful decorations, there is a deeper story behind the tree—one that spans generations, cultures, and traditions. For many, the Christmas tree is not just a decorative centerpiece; it's a symbol of hope, renewal, and connection. It is a reflection of the holiday's spirit, representing both the festive cheer of the season and the deeper meaning of Christmas itself. This chapter explores the story behind the Christmas tree, uncovering the rich history and personal significance it holds for families around the world.

For generations, families have gathered together to choose, decorate, and place their Christmas tree in a place of honor within their homes. The act of selecting a tree, whether it's a grand fir or a humble pine, marks the beginning of the holiday festivities. This tradition, while seemingly simple, holds profound meaning. The tree serves as a canvas for family memories—each ornament and decoration added represents a shared moment, a tradition, or a story that has been passed down over the years. From the first handmade ornament crafted by a child to the vintage baubles that are carefully unpacked year after year, the Christmas tree becomes a living tapestry of family history, connecting past generations with those in the present.

The story behind the tree also extends beyond personal memories and into the realm of symbolism. The evergreen tree, which remains vibrant and green even in the coldest of winters, has long been a symbol of life, endurance, and hope. In many cultures, the tree represents the resilience of the human spirit, a reminder that even in the darkest and coldest times, there is always the potential for growth, renewal, and joy. The Christmas tree, adorned with lights that shine brightly in the winter darkness, becomes a beacon of hope, peace, and goodwill. It is a symbol of light overcoming darkness, of love and warmth shared among family and friends, and of the enduring spirit of Christmas itself.

As we explore the story behind the tree in this chapter, we will uncover not only its historical roots but also the personal connections and memories that make the Christmas tree such an integral part of the holiday experience. It is a story that intertwines tradition, symbolism, and the love shared among families, reminding us of the joy and wonder that come with the holiday season.

A Special Ornament

Among the many ornaments that adorn a Christmas tree, there is often one that stands out—a single, special ornament that carries with it a deeper meaning and holds a place of honor on the tree. It might not be the most glittering or expensive, but it is the one that has a story to tell, one that evokes memories, emotions, and a sense of personal significance. This ornament, whether it's homemade, a family heirloom, or a simple keepsake, becomes more than just a decoration; it becomes a symbol of tradition, love, and the spirit of the season.

For many families, the special ornament is a cherished memento, passed down through generations. It could be a delicate glass bauble from a grandmother's collection, a hand-painted angel crafted by a child many years ago, or a simple wooden star that was carefully carved by a loved one. These ornaments are imbued with stories of the past—each one representing a piece of family history. They might have been given as gifts, created as part of a family tradition, or bought on a special trip, and each one carries with it a unique memory. Over the years, as these ornaments are carefully unwrapped and placed on the tree, they evoke a sense of continuity, reminding family members of those who have come before them and the love and care that have been passed down through the years.

The special ornament is often tied to moments of personal significance, marking important milestones and transitions in a family's life. It could be a silver bell given to a couple on their first Christmas together, a tiny stocking representing the birth of a child, or a heart-shaped ornament celebrating a marriage or an anniversary. These ornaments become markers of time, commemorating moments of joy, growth, and love. They serve as reminders of the milestones that shape our lives, and each time they are hung on the tree, they bring those memories to life. In this way, the special ornament becomes a tangible link between the past and the present, a way to honor and remember the moments that define who we are as individuals and as families.

What makes the special ornament truly remarkable is its ability to evoke emotion. In the quiet moments of decorating the tree, as the lights twinkle and the scent of pine fills the air, the placement of this ornament can trigger a flood of memories. It may remind us of a loved one who is no longer with us, a family tradition that has evolved over the years, or a time of joy and celebration that we hold dear. The ornament serves as a physical representation of these feelings, encapsulating the emotions and experiences that are often difficult to put into words. For families, these ornaments can become a source of comfort and connection, especially during times of loss or change, as they offer a way to keep those memories alive and present.

The beauty of the special ornament is that it does not need to be extravagant to hold meaning. In fact, its simplicity is often what makes it so powerful. It is not about the material value of the ornament, but the love, effort, and memories that are attached to it. Whether it's a handcrafted decoration made by a child or a vintage piece passed down through the generations, the special ornament becomes a precious symbol of the love and connection that define the holiday season. It serves as a reminder that Christmas is not just about the decorations, the gifts, or the meals, but about the moments we share with those we love and the memories we create together.

As families gather each year to decorate their Christmas tree, the special ornament is often the last one to be hung, the finishing touch that completes the display. Its placement marks the culmination of the decorating process, but it also represents the heart of the holiday—a symbol of the love, tradition, and memories that make Christmas so meaningful. The ornament may be small in size, but its significance far exceeds its appearance. It is a reminder of the enduring spirit of Christmas, one that transcends time, distance, and material possessions, connecting us to those we love and to the traditions that shape our lives.

Memories of Christmas Past

As the holiday season approaches each year, there's a certain magic in reflecting on the memories of Christmases gone by. These memories, whether they are joyous, bittersweet, or simply filled with nostalgia, are woven into the very fabric of our lives, shaping how we experience Christmas today. The magic of Christmas past lies in the moments that define our childhood, our family traditions, and the sense of wonder and excitement that the season always brings. It's a time when we gather with loved ones, both present and absent, to recall the stories, the traditions, and the feelings that have made Christmas so special.

For many, Christmas past is filled with the simple joys of childhood—waking up early on Christmas morning, eager to see what Santa has brought, and the thrill of finding a stocking full of surprises. The joy of tearing open presents, the excitement of seeing something you had hoped for, and the wonder of it all have a way of staying with you long after the wrapping paper has been discarded. These memories are timeless, as they capture the innocence and excitement of a season when everything felt new and magical. The images of a sparkling tree, glowing with lights and covered in ornaments, remain vivid in our minds, serving as a symbol of joy and togetherness. In those early years, Christmas is a time of wonder, a season filled with the possibility of magic and delight.

But Christmas past is not just about the gifts or the decorations—it's about the people and the moments shared. The holiday season has a way of bringing family and friends together, and it's these connections that make Christmas truly unforgettable. Memories of sitting around the dinner table, sharing a festive meal, and listening to stories of Christmases from years gone by are cherished moments that stay with us. The laughter of family members, the warmth of close friends gathered in one place, and the shared sense of gratitude and love create an atmosphere that is hard to replicate. These memories remind us that Christmas is not just about what we have, but about the love we give and receive. The food, the gifts, and the decorations all fade, but the relationships we nurture and the moments of connection remain in our hearts.

As the years go by, Christmas takes on new meanings and new traditions. Children grow up, families change, and life moves forward, but the memories of Christmas past continue to serve as a touchstone—a place to return to when we need comfort, inspiration, or just a moment of reflection. Perhaps we remember the voices of loved ones who are no longer with us, or the traditions that have since evolved. Even as we create new memories with those we love, the memories of past Christmases continue to live on, not just in photographs or keepsakes, but in the way we continue to celebrate the season. It is in these memories that we find the roots of our holiday celebrations—where they began and how they have evolved.

Christmas past also often brings with it a sense of longing—a yearning for the simplicity and the wonder of days gone by. There is a bittersweet quality to these memories, as we realize that time moves on and that things will never quite be the same. Yet, in that longing, there is also gratitude—a deep appreciation for the moments we were able to experience and for the people who were part of our holiday celebrations. These memories, even as they stir feelings of loss, are also reminders of the enduring love that exists in our families and communities. They serve as a legacy, one that we can pass on to future generations, ensuring that the spirit of Christmas—its love, its joy, and its sense of wonder—lives on long after the presents have been unwrapped.

In the end, memories of Christmas past are what make the holiday season so meaningful. They are the building blocks of our traditions, the sources of our joy, and the reminders of what truly matters: the people we love, the connections we share, and the moments that take our breath away. Whether they are memories of laughter and joy or moments of quiet reflection, these memories serve as a constant reminder that Christmas is not just a time of celebration, but a time of connection—a time to look back, to remember, and to hold close the things that truly make the season special.

The Tree's Secret
The Tree's Secret

The Christmas tree has long been a symbol of holiday cheer and festive joy, adorned with twinkling lights, shimmering ornaments, and a star or angel perched at its peak. For many, it is the centerpiece of the Christmas celebration, the object around which families gather to exchange gifts, share meals, and create lasting memories. But beneath the vibrant colors and gleaming decorations lies a secret that is often overlooked—a quiet, unspoken magic that makes the Christmas tree much more than a mere decoration. The tree's secret is not in its outward appearance, but in the history it carries, the traditions it embodies, and the stories it quietly tells.

Each ornament on the tree has its own story—a collection of memories passed down from generation to generation, each piece contributing to the tree's hidden narrative. The silver bell that once hung on a grandmother's tree, the handmade ornament from a childhood Christmas, the vintage bauble that has survived decades of holiday seasons—all of these items are more than just festive decorations. They are tokens of the past, each one holding the emotions, experiences, and milestones that have shaped a family's holiday history. The tree becomes a living scrapbook of memories, and every year as it is decorated, new stories are added to its branches. The secret of the tree lies in its ability to carry the past into the present, creating a space where memories are both honored and shared.

The tree also holds the secret of tradition—the way that each family's customs are uniquely intertwined with the holiday season. These traditions, whether they are the same year after year or evolve over time, are passed down from one generation to the next. Perhaps it's the ritual of placing the first ornament on the tree, a moment of significance that marks the beginning of the holiday season. Or maybe it's the story of the tree's selection, where the family comes together to choose the perfect tree from a local farm, each tree representing a new chapter in the family's holiday journey.

These traditions give the tree a secret power—a way of binding family members together through shared experiences, creating a sense of continuity and belonging that extends beyond the season itself.

But perhaps the most profound secret of the Christmas tree is its ability to inspire wonder and reflection. In the quiet moments, when the house is still and the lights on the tree twinkle softly in the dark, the tree becomes a symbol of peace and hope. Its evergreens remind us of life and resilience, standing tall and full of vitality in the coldest months of the year. The lights that illuminate its branches are not just decorations but beacons of joy, warmth, and love, offering a reprieve from the dark winter nights. The star or angel on top, often a symbol of the Christmas story, represents faith and guidance, a reminder of the spiritual significance that Christmas holds for many.

The secret of the tree also lies in its ability to bring people together. Whether it's the act of decorating the tree with loved ones or the shared joy of sitting together beneath its glow, the tree has a way of creating a sense of unity. It draws family members and friends into its orbit, offering a place where memories are made, stories are told, and love is expressed. The act of gathering around the tree and exchanging gifts, or simply sitting in quiet reflection, is an experience that transcends the material aspects of the holiday. The tree becomes a sanctuary of connection, where the true spirit of Christmas is revealed—not in the presents or the festivities, but in the relationships we cultivate and the love we share.

In the end, the tree's secret is a reflection of the holiday season itself. It is not simply about decorations or gifts; it is about the deeper meanings of love, tradition, and connection that Christmas brings. The Christmas tree is a vessel for these meanings, carrying the stories of the past, the hopes of the present, and the promise of the future. As families gather around the tree each year, they not only celebrate the holiday but also honor the legacy of those who came before them, creating new memories that will one day become part of the tree's secret story. The tree, in all its beauty and simplicity, stands as a testament to the enduring power of love, tradition, and the quiet magic that makes Christmas so special.

Chapter 5

The Gift of Love

At the heart of Christmas lies the most precious gift of all—the gift of love. While presents may be exchanged, decorations hung, and festive meals shared, it is the love we give and receive that truly defines the season. Christmas is a time when we are reminded of the importance of love in all its forms—love for family, for friends, for strangers, and for ourselves. The act of giving love transcends material gifts, creating a warmth that fills the heart and nurtures the soul. In this chapter, we explore how the gift of love, though intangible, is the most enduring and meaningful part of the holiday season.

The gift of love is not bound by any expectation or condition. It's not measured by how expensive the gift is or how grand the gesture appears; it's measured by the depth of feeling and sincerity behind it. Love can be expressed in countless ways—through a heartfelt note, a simple act of kindness, or the gift of time. It's the thoughtfulness that goes into understanding someone's needs, the willingness to offer comfort when it's needed most, and the ability to give without expecting anything in return. This chapter will explore how the gift of love is the foundation of all other gifts, imbuing the holiday season with its true spirit.

At Christmas, love becomes a bridge that connects us all. Whether it's the love shared among family members gathered around the dinner table, the love shown through acts of charity, or the love we extend to others during times of hardship, it creates a bond that transcends all boundaries. The power of love is what makes

Christmas such a transformative time—a time to reflect on our relationships, heal past wounds, and open our hearts to those around us. As we look at the gift of love in this chapter, we will uncover its ability to heal, unite, and bring joy to our lives, making this season not just a celebration of giving, but a reminder of the love that surrounds us all.

Rekindling Old Bonds

The holiday season has a unique way of bringing people together, sparking moments of connection that can heal old wounds and rekindle relationships that may have faded over time. As Christmas approaches, many find themselves reflecting on the relationships that have shaped their lives, the connections that have been strained by time, distance, or misunderstandings. There is something about the spirit of Christmas that encourages forgiveness, understanding, and the renewal of old bonds. It is a season not only for giving and celebration but also for reconciliation and reflection.

Rekindling old bonds often begins with a moment of introspection—remembering the joy, love, and laughter shared in the past. Life moves fast, and in the hustle and bustle of everyday responsibilities, it's easy for relationships to slip through the cracks. Friendships and family ties that once flourished may begin to fade, not out of malice, but simply because of life's many distractions. Christmas offers a moment to pause and consider the connections that have been lost or neglected. It reminds us of the importance of these bonds and invites us to reach out and rekindle them. The season creates a space for re-engagement, where past grievances or misunderstandings can be set aside in favor of reconciliation. The act of reaching out, whether through a phone call, a heartfelt message, or an invitation to reconnect, opens the door to healing and restoration.

One of the most beautiful aspects of rekindling old bonds during the holiday season is the shared history that binds people together.

Family and friends who may have been apart for years have the chance to remember the times they spent together, the milestones they celebrated, and the love they once shared. These shared memories serve as a reminder of the connection that existed in the past, making it easier to rebuild what was lost. In many cases, rekindling old bonds is about rediscovering those common threads that once united two people—whether it's a shared love for a particular tradition, a mutual respect for each other's values, or simply the understanding that despite time apart, the love they once shared is still present. These memories, which may have been dormant for years, resurface in the warmth of the holiday season, making it the perfect time to reconnect and rebuild.

Rekindling old bonds isn't always easy. It requires vulnerability, honesty, and a willingness to forgive past hurts. Sometimes, it means letting go of old grudges, accepting imperfections, and embracing the idea that people change over time. Christmas provides the perfect backdrop for this kind of emotional healing. The season's focus on love, compassion, and new beginnings offers a natural opportunity to approach past relationships with a fresh perspective. Whether it's a sibling who has drifted away, a friend who's been out of touch, or a family member with whom you've lost contact, reaching out during Christmas creates an atmosphere of openness and renewal. The very act of extending a hand, even if it's tentative at first, can spark a meaningful conversation that leads to understanding and forgiveness.

What's even more beautiful is that rekindling old bonds is often a two-way street. While one person may take the first step, it is in the response of the other person that healing truly begins. Reconnecting with someone from the past is a reminder that relationships are not one-sided; they are built on mutual understanding, trust, and care. When two people reach across the divide, they can rediscover the love and respect that once defined their relationship, finding joy in each other's company once again.

This Christmas, as you reflect on the relationships that matter most to you, consider the power of rekindling old bonds. Whether it's reaching out to a long-lost friend, reconnecting with a distant family member, or healing a fractured relationship, the holiday season offers a unique opportunity for renewal. In rekindling these connections, you not only restore relationships but also reignite the spirit of Christmas—one of love, forgiveness, and the joy of being together. The bonds we nurture during the holidays become part of our legacy, creating new memories that will last for years to come, enriching our lives and the lives of those we love.

Heartfelt Conversations

Christmas is a time when the heart seems to open a little wider, and the soul feels more attuned to the people around us. Amid the celebrations, the gifts, and the festivities, there is an undeniable magic in the quiet moments of connection. One of the most profound aspects of the holiday season is the opportunity it provides for heartfelt conversations—those deep, meaningful exchanges that foster understanding, connection, and emotional healing. These conversations, often sparked by the warmth of the season, can reignite relationships, heal old wounds, and strengthen the bonds between family members and friends.

At its core, a heartfelt conversation is one that comes from a place of authenticity. It is a conversation that is driven by a genuine desire to connect, to share what's on our hearts, and to listen with empathy and understanding. The holiday season, with its emphasis on family, togetherness, and gratitude, creates the perfect environment for such exchanges. Whether it's a quiet conversation by the fireplace, a phone call with an old friend, or a heartfelt discussion over a holiday meal, these moments of connection allow us to share our joys, our struggles, and our hopes for the future. In these conversations, we open ourselves to each other in a way that can be both comforting and healing.

Heartfelt conversations are often born out of shared experiences, whether they are positive or challenging. Perhaps it's a reflection on the highs and lows of the past year, or a chance to reminisce about shared memories from Christmases gone by. These conversations provide an opportunity for people to express their gratitude, to acknowledge the difficulties they've faced, and to celebrate the growth and lessons learned along the way. For some, the holiday season is a time to share personal stories, to confess things left unsaid, or to seek forgiveness for past mistakes. The intimacy of these exchanges allows people to be vulnerable, to show their true selves without fear of judgment. It is in these moments of honesty and vulnerability that real healing takes place—when the walls come down, and the connection deepens.

One of the beautiful things about heartfelt conversations is that they have the power to create lasting memories. While gifts and material presents are often fleeting, the impact of a meaningful conversation can last a lifetime. Whether it's a heartfelt thank you, an expression of love, or the sharing of a deeply personal story, these conversations leave an indelible mark on our hearts. They become memories that we carry with us, replaying them in our minds in moments of quiet reflection. A conversation that reassures us, that makes us feel understood and appreciated, can change the way we view ourselves and others. It is a gift that cannot be wrapped or bought, but one that is cherished far beyond the holiday season.

At Christmas, these conversations often serve as a reminder of what truly matters. In a world that can sometimes feel fast-paced and distracted, the act of sitting down with someone and truly listening to them is a rare and precious gift. Heartfelt conversations bring us back to the core of human connection—love, empathy, and understanding. They allow us to remember what it means to be fully present with the people we care about. In sharing our thoughts, our feelings, and our stories, we build a deeper sense of intimacy and trust, fostering relationships that will endure long after the Christmas season has passed.

The gift of a heartfelt conversation is one of the most meaningful aspects of the holiday season. It is in these conversations that we find the true essence of Christmas: love, connection, and the joy of being together. So often, we are caught up in the frenzy of shopping, wrapping gifts, and preparing meals, but it is the quiet, unspoken moments—those exchanges of words that come straight from the heart—that truly define the season. They are the moments that remind us that the best gifts are not always found under the tree, but in the bonds we share and the conversations that bring us closer together.

A Present Beyond Measure

At Christmas, the act of giving gifts is a cherished tradition, one that brings joy and excitement to both the giver and the receiver. The anticipation of finding the perfect present, wrapped in shiny paper and adorned with a bow, fills the air with excitement. Yet, beyond the material presents exchanged, there exists a gift far more precious and meaningful—a present that transcends any object or tangible item. This gift is the gift of love, time, and presence. It is a present that cannot be measured by price or wrapped in paper, but one that leaves a lasting impact far beyond any material possession. The gift of genuine connection, of offering oneself fully to another, is the present that lasts the longest and touches the heart most deeply.

The present beyond measure is the gift of time. In a world that is constantly moving, where the demands of work, family, and daily life often leave little room for meaningful connections, the gift of time is one of the most precious offerings we can give. When we give someone our undivided attention, when we sit down and truly listen, when we spend time with someone without distraction, we are offering them a part of ourselves that is irreplaceable. Time is a finite resource; we can always buy more gifts, but we cannot get back time once it is spent. To give someone the gift of our time is to show them that they are worth our attention, that they matter enough to be prioritized over everything else. Whether it's sitting with an elderly relative, sharing a meal with a friend, or simply being present for a loved one, the gift of time strengthens relationships and creates lasting memories.

Another immeasurable present is the gift of empathy. At Christmas, the spirit of compassion and understanding is amplified. The act of truly seeing someone for who they are, understanding their joys and struggles, and offering emotional support is a gift that cannot be wrapped in a box. Empathy is the ability to connect with another person's experience and provide comfort, reassurance, and love. It is a gift that transcends all boundaries, one that can heal wounds, ease burdens, and uplift the spirit. At Christmas, when we extend our hearts to others, when we listen with compassion and offer a shoulder to lean on, we are giving a present that no amount of money can buy—a present that is deeply transformative for both the giver and the receiver.

The present beyond measure is also found in the act of forgiveness. During the holiday season, emotions are often heightened, and relationships can be tested. The gift of forgiveness—whether it's letting go of past hurts, offering a second chance, or making amends—has the power to heal rifts that may have existed for years. Christmas is a time to reflect on the values of love, kindness, and reconciliation, and what better way to embody these values than through the act of forgiveness? By offering forgiveness, we free ourselves from the weight of resentment and open the door to a renewed connection with others. It's a gift that not only heals relationships but also lifts the burden of emotional pain, allowing both parties to move forward with peace and grace.

Perhaps the most enduring present beyond measure is the gift of unconditional love. Love is the force that binds families together, that builds strong friendships, and that fuels acts of kindness and generosity. Unconditional love is not bound by conditions or expectations; it is a love that is freely given, without asking for anything in return. This kind of love is present in a mother's embrace, in a partner's support, and in a friend's loyalty. It is in the words spoken in times of need, in the comforting presence when words fail, and in the shared laughter that echoes through years of memories. The gift of unconditional love is the foundation of every other meaningful gift we give. It is the gift that gives us the strength to endure hardships, the courage to face challenges, and the joy to celebrate life's blessings.

The present beyond measure is one that doesn't fit into a box or come with a price tag. It is the gift of who we are to one another—the gift of our time, our empathy, our forgiveness, and our love. This Christmas, as we exchange material gifts, let us also remember that the most meaningful presents are those that cannot be measured, wrapped, or bought. They are the gifts that come straight from the heart, the gifts that leave a lasting impact on the soul, and the gifts that define what the holiday season is truly about: love, connection, and the joy of being present with one another.

Chapter 6
A Snowy Christmas Morning

There's something truly magical about a snowy Christmas morning, as if the world has been transformed overnight into a peaceful winter wonderland. The ground is blanketed in fresh, untouched snow, and the air feels crisp and clean, carrying a sense of quiet serenity. As the first light of dawn breaks, the gentle glow from the Christmas tree seems even brighter against the backdrop of the snow-covered landscape outside. The world feels still, as though time has slowed, allowing families to bask in the warmth and joy of the season. In these moments, the magic of Christmas is not just in the gifts under the tree, but in the pure beauty of the morning itself.

For children, a snowy Christmas morning is filled with anticipation and excitement. The thrill of running downstairs to see what Santa has left behind, the joy of discovering stockings filled with treats, and the wonder of seeing the snow outside make it a day like no other. The snowflakes, drifting lazily to the ground, add an extra layer of wonder to the scene. For a child, it's a world of possibilities—sledding down the hills, building snowmen, or simply catching snowflakes on their tongues. A snowy Christmas morning invites play, adventure, and pure, unbridled joy, as families gather to enjoy the beauty of nature and the warmth of each other's company.

But a snowy Christmas morning is also a time of quiet reflection, where moments of peace and stillness offer a chance to pause and take in the blessings of the season. As the family gathers for breakfast or settles by the fire, the peacefulness of the snow outside mirrors the calm in their hearts. The soft falling snow serves as a reminder of the stillness and purity that Christmas brings—a time to reflect on the love shared, the memories made, and the hope that the season embodies. In the quiet of the morning, with snow gently falling outside, the true spirit of Christmas is felt: a time for connection, renewal, and the joy of being together.

The Beauty of a Silent Winter

Winter often carries with it a unique silence, a stillness that seems to wrap the world in a quiet embrace. The beauty of a silent winter is not found in the noise of bustling streets or the rush of holiday activities, but rather in the profound calm that descends as the cold weather takes hold. There is something undeniably peaceful about the way winter hushes the world, transforming the landscape into a serene and almost sacred space. Snow falls softly, covering the earth like a blanket, muffling sounds and creating a world that feels both expansive and intimate. In these moments of silence, the beauty of winter reveals itself in its purest form.

One of the most striking features of a silent winter is the way it enhances the natural world. The snow, which falls quietly from the sky, transforms ordinary scenes into extraordinary works of art. Trees, once bare and dark against the autumn sky, become delicate silhouettes, their branches heavy with snow, each one glistening like a work of glass. Fields, roads, and parks are draped in a blanket of white, softening the sharp edges of the world and turning it into a place of gentle curves and subtle contrasts. In the silence of winter, the details of the landscape come alive—the patterns in the snow created by the wind, the delicate frost on the windows, the way the light reflects off the ice, and the stillness of the frozen lakes. Everything seems suspended in time, as if the world itself is holding its breath.

This silence allows us to experience nature in a new way. The usual clamor of life—the noise of traffic, the chatter of people, the hum of everyday existence—seems to fade away, leaving room for introspection and quiet appreciation. The absence of sound in a winter landscape creates a space for reflection. It's as though the world becomes clearer, more focused, as we are invited to slow down and observe the beauty that often goes unnoticed in the hustle and bustle of daily life. It's in the quiet moments that we can truly hear the whispers of nature—whether it's the soft crunch of boots on snow, the rustling of distant trees, or the occasional chirp of a winter bird. These sounds, when they do emerge, seem amplified against the backdrop of winter's silence, offering a deeper connection to the world around us.

The beauty of a silent winter also lies in its ability to foster a sense of inner peace. In a time when the world can feel overwhelming, when we are constantly bombarded by the noise of modern life, the stillness of winter offers a reprieve. The cold, crisp air, the softness of the snow, and the quiet of the surroundings create a calming atmosphere that invites us to pause, to reflect, and to find solace. There is something grounding about walking through a quiet winter forest, or sitting by a frosted window, watching the snow fall. In those moments, we are reminded of the quiet strength and resilience that winter itself represents. Winter may seem barren on the surface, but beneath the cold exterior, it is a season of deep rest, rejuvenation, and growth, just waiting for the spring to bring it to life again.

Furthermore, the beauty of a silent winter is not just visual or physical—it's emotional. The season invites us to connect with those around us in a way that is often more meaningful than during other times of the year. As we gather inside, away from the cold, we are encouraged to connect with our loved ones in deeper, more intimate ways. Whether it's sharing a warm cup of tea by the fire, reading a favorite holiday book, or simply being present with one another, the quiet of winter creates a backdrop for closeness and connection. It is in these still moments that we often find the time to share stories, reflect on memories, and cherish the bonds we have with others.

In essence, the beauty of a silent winter lies in its ability to transform the world into a peaceful, reflective space where nature and humanity are brought closer together. It is a season that invites us to pause, to appreciate the quiet moments, and to find beauty in stillness. The calm that winter brings allows us to see the world differently—more clearly, more slowly, and with a deeper sense of gratitude. As the snow falls softly and the world becomes hushed, we are reminded that sometimes the most beautiful things are the ones we experience in silence.

Surprises Await

Christmas is a time of anticipation, a season when the promise of surprises fills the air with excitement and wonder. Whether it's the thrill of unwrapping presents or the joy of unexpected moments that seem to materialize out of nowhere, the holiday season has a way of delivering surprises that make the season unforgettable. These surprises often arrive in ways we least expect—small moments of joy, acts of kindness, or even unexpected visitors—that remind us of the magic and beauty of Christmas. It's a time when the ordinary becomes extraordinary, when the mundane is infused with a sense of wonder, and when surprises truly await around every corner.

One of the most magical aspects of Christmas is the surprise of giving and receiving. It's not just about the material gifts, though they certainly play a big role in the holiday cheer. It's the thoughtfulness and care that go into choosing a present for someone special. The joy of finding the perfect gift, something that truly reflects the recipient's personality, interests, or needs, can be a delightful surprise in itself. It's the moment when you see the look of genuine appreciation on someone's face as they unwrap a gift that you spent hours searching for, or the feeling of warmth that fills your heart when you receive a gift that shows how much someone truly cares for you. In these moments, Christmas surprises remind us that the best gifts are often the ones that come from the heart, and they bring with them a sense of connection and love that lasts far beyond the holiday season.

But the surprises of Christmas aren't always material. Sometimes, they come in the form of unexpected visits, unplanned gatherings, or spontaneous moments of joy. A knock on the door to find an old friend or a long-lost relative standing there, ready to celebrate the season with you, is one of the most heartwarming surprises that Christmas can bring. These unexpected visits—whether from family, friends, or even strangers—remind us of the true spirit of the holiday: connection, compassion, and the joy of being with those we love. Whether it's an impromptu carol sing-along, a surprise dinner party, or simply a quiet moment shared by the fire, these surprises add a layer of depth and meaning to the holiday, making it feel even more special and memorable.

Sometimes, the surprises of Christmas come in the form of serendipitous moments that seem to carry the magic of the season. Perhaps it's a snowstorm that unexpectedly blankets the streets, creating the perfect opportunity for a cozy night in with loved ones. Or maybe it's a sudden change in plans that leads to an unforgettable experience—like a spontaneous trip, a surprise adventure, or an unplanned opportunity to make new memories. These surprises remind us that life, much like Christmas, is full of unexpected moments that can turn the ordinary into something extraordinary. They encourage us to let go of rigid expectations and embrace the beauty of the unexpected, knowing that sometimes the best moments are the ones we don't plan for at all.

In the hustle and bustle of the holiday season, it's easy to get caught up in the details—the shopping, the cooking, the organizing—but Christmas surprises offer us a chance to pause and appreciate the spontaneous, the unscripted, and the magical moments that make the holiday truly special. Whether it's a thoughtful gesture, a surprise visit, or a moment of quiet reflection, these surprises invite us to experience Christmas with open hearts and minds, ready to embrace whatever comes our way. The holiday season, with all its surprises, reminds us that there is always room for wonder, and that life's most meaningful gifts often arrive when we least expect them.

Ultimately, the surprises that await at Christmas are not just about gifts or events—they're about the spirit of the season itself. They are reminders of the joy and love that fill the air, the moments of togetherness that make us feel truly connected, and the beauty of a season that invites us to look beyond the ordinary and see the magic in everything. In the end, Christmas surprises aren't just about the big moments; they are about the little things—the unexpected joys, the unplanned connections, and the quiet moments of reflection—that make the holiday so memorable and meaningful.

The Wonder of Childhood

The wonder of childhood is a special kind of magic, a sense of awe and excitement that colors the world in vibrant hues of possibility. For children, everything around them is new, fresh, and filled with potential, especially during the holiday season. Christmas, with its twinkling lights, festive sounds, and the promise of surprise, becomes a time when that wonder is heightened. The season brings to life the dreams and fantasies that children hold close, allowing them to experience the world through a lens of pure joy and limitless imagination. The wonder of childhood, particularly at Christmas, is a gift—one that reminds us of the innocence, excitement, and sense of magic that we can often forget as we grow older.

At the heart of this wonder is the joy of discovery. For children, Christmas is a time when everything seems possible. The thought of Santa Claus traveling the world on Christmas Eve, reindeer flying through the sky, and the anticipation of presents appearing under the tree fills the days leading up to the holiday with excitement. There is an innocence in believing in these magical stories—the way a child's eyes light up with the thrill of the unknown, their hearts full of hope and anticipation. The rituals of Christmas—the hanging of stockings, the decorating of the tree, the baking of cookies—become part of a larger story that they are actively involved in, and the excitement they feel becomes contagious to everyone around them. The wonder of childhood at Christmas is not just about the tangible gifts received but about the larger narrative of joy and magic that surrounds the season.

The beauty of the wonder of childhood at Christmas is also found in the small details—the way a child's face lights up when they see the first snowfall of the season or the sense of awe when they see the Christmas tree glowing in the living room for the first time. These moments, though simple, are infused with an energy that only a child can experience. The decorations that adults might take for granted—the sparkling lights, the ornaments hanging on the tree—become objects of fascination and wonder for young ones. They are not just objects but part of the story of Christmas, pieces of a puzzle that children eagerly put together in their minds. The world, for them, is full of surprises and wonders, and Christmas magnifies this sense of magic, making the holiday a time when every moment seems extraordinary.

In childhood, Christmas also brings with it the thrill of anticipation, which fuels the wonder of the season. Children eagerly await the arrival of Christmas morning, counting down the days with excited energy. The act of waking up to presents under the tree, stockings filled with treats, and the possibility of something special being hidden behind the wrapping paper creates a sense of joy that only a child can fully understand. The wonder of childhood at Christmas is found in the excitement of the unknown, in the belief that anything is possible. It's a time when dreams come alive, when the magic of the season is embodied in every surprise, every twinkling light, and every moment spent with family.

Yet, the wonder of childhood is also something deeply personal. It's not just about the external magic of the season but about the internal feeling that Christmas brings—a sense of belonging, of warmth, and of unconditional love. For children, Christmas is a time when the people they love come together, creating a sense of security and happiness that is deeply felt. The joy of opening presents is enhanced by the love shared with family, the laughter, and the togetherness that fills the room. These moments of connection, of sharing in the joy of the season with others, become a part of the wonder of childhood, teaching children the true meaning of love, generosity, and the beauty of giving.

The wonder of childhood at Christmas is fleeting, but it's something that stays with us throughout our lives. It shapes how we view the world, the value we place on family, and the excitement we feel when we experience the unexpected. As we grow older, we may lose some of the innocence that comes with childhood, but the memories of that wonder—those moments of pure joy, belief, and excitement—continue to live within us, shaping our sense of wonder even as adults. Christmas, in all its magic, serves as a reminder of the beauty of childhood and the importance of holding onto that sense of wonder, even as life becomes more complex. The wonder of childhood is a gift that, when embraced, can bring joy and meaning to every holiday season, and to every day that follows.

Chapter 7

Joy Found in the Little Things

In the whirlwind of the holiday season, where the hustle and bustle of shopping, cooking, and celebrations often dominate, it is easy to overlook the simple moments that bring true joy. Yet, the real magic of Christmas lies not in grand gestures or extravagant gifts, but in the small, seemingly insignificant moments that, when taken together, create the essence of the season. It is in the quiet moments—watching the first snowflakes fall, sharing a laugh over a holiday meal, or simply sitting in silence with loved ones—that the greatest joys of Christmas are found. In this chapter, we explore how it's the little things that bring the deepest happiness, and how these simple acts of connection and gratitude define the spirit of the season.

The joy found in the little things is often rooted in the everyday experiences we share with those we love. It's in the warmth of a cup of hot cocoa shared on a cold evening, the laughter of family members as they tell stories by the fireplace, or the comfort of wrapping yourself in a cozy blanket as you watch holiday movies. These moments, small as they may seem, become the heart of the Christmas experience. They are the building blocks of memories, the pieces that come together to create a picture of what the season truly means. The beauty of these little things is that they are accessible to everyone, regardless of where they are or what they have. It is not the material that matters, but the joy and connection that these moments foster.

What makes the little things even more special is their ability to bring us back to what really matters—the people around us and the love we share. The simplest of gestures, whether it's a kind word, a shared smile, or a thoughtful touch, can have a profound impact. These small acts of kindness and connection build the foundation for deeper relationships and a more meaningful celebration. In a season often focused on gifts and outward displays, the little things remind us that the true spirit of Christmas is about fostering connections, embracing gratitude, and celebrating the joy that comes from simply being present with those who matter most. In this chapter, we celebrate these moments, recognizing them as the true essence of Christmas joy.

The Laughter of Children

The laughter of children during Christmas is one of the most pure and joyous sounds that fills the air. It is a sound that reflects the true essence of the holiday season—innocence, excitement, and uncontained joy. Children, with their wide eyes full of wonder and their hearts brimming with hope, experience Christmas with a sense of awe that makes every moment seem like a gift. Their laughter is infectious, spreading joy not just in the rooms they occupy but to everyone within earshot, reminding us of the simple pleasures that come with this time of year. It is a laughter that resonates with the magic of the season, a laughter that echoes in our hearts long after the sounds have faded.

The laughter of children at Christmas is often sparked by the smallest of moments. Perhaps it's the excitement of waking up to discover stockings filled with treats or the thrill of tearing open presents to find something they've eagerly hoped for. It could be the joy of seeing the Christmas tree for the first time, its lights twinkling and ornaments shining, or the wonder of catching a glimpse of Santa's sleigh flying through the sky. For children, Christmas is a time of boundless imagination, where the ordinary becomes extraordinary and where every new discovery brings with it the promise of more joy. Their laughter flows naturally from this sense of wonder—the thrill of believing in something magical and the sheer delight in sharing those magical moments with others.

What makes the laughter of children even more special is its ability to remind us of the beauty of the present moment. As adults, we often find ourselves lost in the stress of preparing for the holiday season—the shopping, the cooking, the organizing—and forget to embrace the simplicity and joy that Christmas brings. Yet, when we hear the laughter of a child, we are reminded to slow down and take in the wonder of it all. It is in these moments that we are able to reconnect with the magic of the season, to remember that Christmas isn't about the perfect meal or the most expensive gift, but about the simple, fleeting moments of joy that make this time of year so special.

The laughter of children also symbolizes the hope and renewal that Christmas brings. Children experience the holiday with an openness and authenticity that we often lose as we grow older. Their laughter is a reflection of the world they see—a world where anything is possible, where kindness and generosity abound, and where love is at the heart of it all. When children laugh, they invite us to embrace that same sense of wonder, to approach life with a renewed sense of hope, and to find joy in the little things. This laughter serves as a reminder that Christmas is not just about what we receive, but about what we give—to others and to ourselves. It is a call to be present, to embrace the people we love, and to celebrate the beauty of life's simplest pleasures.

In many ways, the laughter of children is the heartbeat of Christmas. It is the sound that signals the beginning of the holiday season, that fills the air with anticipation, and that marks the joy and excitement of shared experiences. The laughter of children reminds us of the true meaning of Christmas—that it is a time to come together, to appreciate what we have, and to celebrate the joy of being with those we love. It's in their laughter that we find the joy of the season reflected back to us, pure and unfiltered, a gift that continues to warm our hearts year after year.

A Simple Feast

There is something profoundly beautiful about a simple feast, especially during the Christmas season. In a time when extravagant meals and elaborate spreads are often the focus of the holiday, the joy of a simple feast reminds us that Christmas is not about abundance or excess, but about sharing what we have with those we love. A simple feast doesn't need to be elaborate or expensive; it's about the warmth of togetherness, the love that goes into preparing the meal, and the joy of sitting down to enjoy it with family and friends. It's in these moments of simplicity that the true spirit of Christmas shines brightest.

A simple feast doesn't require a table full of dishes or the most expensive ingredients. Instead, it is made meaningful by the care and thoughtfulness put into the preparation. Perhaps it's a warm bowl of homemade soup, freshly baked bread, or a roast that has been carefully seasoned and slow-cooked to perfection. These meals, though humble, are a reflection of the time and love that goes into creating them. There is beauty in the simplicity of a home-cooked meal shared around a table. It's not the complexity of the dishes that matters, but the comfort and nourishment they provide, both physically and emotionally. The joy of gathering around a simple feast is in the act of being together, in the conversation, laughter, and connection that flows freely as everyone enjoys the meal.

The simplicity of the feast also allows for an appreciation of the small things—the aroma of freshly cooked food, the warmth of the kitchen, and the way the light dances across the table. It's in the simple act of preparing the meal, whether it's peeling vegetables, stirring a pot, or setting the table, that the heart of Christmas is revealed. In these moments, we can slow down and focus on what truly matters. A simple feast, free from the distractions of the outside world, becomes a celebration of the present moment. It invites us to cherish the time spent with loved ones, to savor the flavors of the food, and to appreciate the little things that make the season special.

Moreover, a simple feast often brings with it a sense of gratitude. It's not about the amount of food on the table but the appreciation for what we have. In a world where excess is often the norm, the simplicity of a humble meal reminds us of the value of contentment and thankfulness. It encourages us to focus on the blessings we have rather than what we lack. Whether it's a small family dinner or a modest gathering of friends, the act of sharing a meal becomes a symbol of gratitude for the abundance, however simple, that we experience. The conversations around the table, the shared smiles, and the warmth of the meal are gifts in themselves.

The beauty of a simple feast is also found in its ability to bring people together. When we gather to share food, it's not just about nourishing the body—it's about nourishing the relationships that matter most. A simple feast allows for conversation to flow, for stories to be told, and for connections to be strengthened. It's in the shared experience of breaking bread together that we find a sense of belonging and unity. Whether the meal is large or small, simple or extravagant, it is the act of coming together to celebrate that gives it meaning.

In the end, a simple feast is a reminder that Christmas is not about perfection or excess. It is about the joy of being together, of sharing what we have, and of appreciating the beauty of the season in its simplest form. The love and connection that a simple feast fosters are what make it so powerful. It's not the grand gestures or lavish meals that define Christmas; it's the warmth, the love, and the joy found in the simplest moments shared around a table. A simple feast becomes a celebration of what truly matters: the people we hold dear, the memories we create, and the love that fills the room.

Moments of Gratitude

Christmas is a time of giving and receiving, of celebration and togetherness, but at its core, it is also a time to reflect on the many blessings in our lives. The holiday season offers a unique opportunity to pause and express gratitude for all that we have— whether it's the love of family, the warmth of home, the gifts we share, or simply the gift of life itself. In a world that often moves too quickly, the moments of gratitude that arise during Christmas serve as a gentle reminder to slow down, appreciate the present, and acknowledge the abundance in our lives, both big and small.

One of the most profound aspects of Christmas is the opportunity it gives us to express our gratitude to those who matter most. It's a time when we come together with family and friends, and in these moments of connection, we are reminded of the importance of the relationships we have nurtured throughout the year. Whether it's a heartfelt thank-you for a thoughtful gift, a warm hug shared with a loved one, or simply an expression of appreciation for the time spent together, these moments of gratitude help us reconnect with what truly matters. The simple act of acknowledging the efforts and love of those around us brings a sense of warmth and fulfillment that no material gift can replicate. Gratitude strengthens relationships, deepens bonds, and creates a shared sense of joy that elevates the Christmas experience.

Beyond the people in our lives, Christmas also encourages us to reflect on the blessings we often take for granted. In the midst of gift-giving, festive meals, and celebrations, there is a quiet reminder to appreciate the simple things that bring us comfort and joy. The warmth of a home, the health of loved ones, and the freedom to enjoy the holiday season are all gifts that we can sometimes overlook. Christmas serves as a time to pause and reflect on these everyday blessings, acknowledging the abundance that exists in our lives. In moments of quiet reflection, we recognize that gratitude isn't just about the grand gestures but also the small, everyday moments that make life worth living—the laughter of children, the peace of a snowy evening, or the shared joy of a simple meal. These moments, though often fleeting, are the building blocks of happiness and contentment.

Christmas also invites us to be grateful for the challenges we have faced and the lessons we have learned. While the holiday season is often associated with joy and celebration, it can also be a time to reflect on the struggles and hardships of the past year. Moments of difficulty, loss, or heartache may feel heavy, but they offer us the chance to grow, to develop resilience, and to appreciate the strength we have gained. In these moments of gratitude, we can find the wisdom that comes from overcoming adversity, the lessons that life has taught us, and the sense of peace that comes with acceptance. By acknowledging the difficult moments alongside the joyful ones, we create a fuller, richer sense of gratitude—one that encompasses both the light and the dark and allows us to embrace the fullness of life.

As we gather with loved ones this Christmas, we are given the gift of time—the time to reflect, to connect, and to be present. In these moments, gratitude naturally arises. It is in the shared laughter, the quiet moments of connection, and the celebration of love that we realize the true meaning of Christmas. It is not in the number of presents we receive, the decorations we hang, or the meals we prepare, but in the moments of gratitude that we share with others. These moments are the heart of the holiday season, reminding us that what truly matters are the relationships we cultivate, the love we give, and the appreciation we feel for the blessings in our lives.

In the end, Christmas is a time to pause and reflect on the many gifts we have received throughout the year, not just in material form but in the richness of our lives—the people we love, the experiences that have shaped us, and the moments of joy and peace that make life meaningful. Moments of gratitude help us slow down, appreciate the present, and find joy in the small, everyday blessings that surround us. It's through these moments that we connect with the true spirit of Christmas—a spirit of love, appreciation, and a deep recognition of the beauty of life itself.

Chapter 8

The Meaning of Christmas

Christmas is a holiday that resonates with people around the world in many different ways, yet its deeper meaning transcends cultures, traditions, and customs. At its core, Christmas is a time of reflection—a moment to pause and connect with what truly matters. While the holiday is often associated with gift-giving, decorations, and festive meals, the true essence of Christmas lies in the spirit of love, generosity, and hope that it embodies. In this chapter, we will explore the deeper meaning of Christmas, beyond the material aspects, and reflect on the values that make this season so special and transformative.

For many, Christmas is a time to reconnect with family, friends, and loved ones. It is a celebration of togetherness, of shared memories, and of the bonds that hold us together. At its heart, Christmas is about relationships—both with those around us and with ourselves. The holiday season encourages us to slow down and appreciate the time spent with others, to offer our love freely, and to express our gratitude for the people who bring joy and meaning to our lives. It is a reminder that the connections we nurture are the true gifts of the season, and that love and compassion are the greatest treasures we can offer.

At a deeper level, the meaning of Christmas is rooted in the values of compassion, hope, and renewal. For many, it is a time to reflect on the teachings of kindness and selflessness, embracing the spirit of giving without expectation. The story of the birth of Jesus Christ, the light that came into the world to bring peace and goodwill, serves as a reminder of the transformative power of love and forgiveness. Christmas calls us to open our hearts to others, to extend kindness to those in need, and to celebrate the hope that the season brings—a hope for a better world, filled with compassion and understanding. Through this lens, Christmas is not just a holiday, but a way of living—one that encourages us to embody the values of love, generosity, and peace, not just during the season, but throughout the entire year.

Reflections on the Season

As the year draws to a close, the Christmas season offers a unique opportunity for reflection. The holiday season, with its festive cheer and moments of togetherness, invites us to pause and take stock of the year that has passed. It is a time when we look inward, considering the lessons learned, the challenges faced, and the blessings we have received. Amidst the hustle and bustle, the parties, the shopping, and the decorations, Christmas offers a quiet space to reflect on the deeper meaning of the season and its significance in our lives.

One of the most powerful aspects of Christmas is its ability to bring us into the present moment. In the midst of our busy lives, it is easy to become caught up in the future or to dwell on the past. Yet, Christmas encourages us to focus on the here and now. The simple act of gathering with loved ones, sharing a meal, or exchanging thoughtful gifts brings us back to what truly matters. These moments of connection allow us to appreciate the present, to savor the time spent with family and friends, and to acknowledge the joy that exists in the everyday. It is through these small but meaningful interactions that we find the true spirit of Christmas—not in the material aspects of the holiday, but in the relationships we cherish and the time we spend nurturing them.

Christmas also provides a time for gratitude. The holiday season encourages us to reflect on all that we have—our family, our health, our home—and to express our appreciation for the blessings in our lives. It is a season that reminds us of the importance of giving thanks, not just for the good things but for the challenges as well. Each year brings its share of trials and tribulations, yet it is often through these experiences that we grow the most. As we reflect on the past year, we may realize that the hardships we faced helped us to become stronger, more compassionate, and more resilient. Christmas offers an opportunity to express gratitude not only for the joys we've experienced but also for the lessons we've learned and the growth we've achieved.

Another key element of reflection during the Christmas season is the theme of renewal. Christmas symbolizes the birth of new possibilities—the hope of a new year, a new beginning. It is a reminder that no matter what has happened in the past, we are given the opportunity to start fresh. Just as the birth of Jesus brought hope and light into the world, Christmas offers us a chance to embrace the future with optimism and faith. It is a time to set new intentions, to consider what we want to cultivate in the coming year, and to reflect on the changes we would like to make. The end of the year provides a natural point for self-reflection, allowing us to assess our lives and determine how we want to move forward with intention and purpose.

As we reflect on the season, it is also important to acknowledge the universal values that Christmas embodies—love, compassion, kindness, and generosity. These values transcend cultural and religious boundaries, serving as a reminder of the common humanity that binds us all together. Christmas calls us to open our hearts, to extend compassion to others, and to spread goodwill wherever we go. It reminds us that the greatest gift we can give is love—the love we offer to our families, our communities, and even to strangers. It is through these acts of kindness that we can make the world a better place, one small gesture at a time.

In essence, Christmas is not just a holiday but a season of reflection—a time to pause and appreciate the many blessings in our lives, to express gratitude for both the good and the challenging, and to embrace the hope and renewal that comes with a new year. It is a time to reconnect with the values that matter most and to reflect on the relationships that give our lives meaning. As we look back on the year that has passed, let us carry forward the lessons learned, the love shared, and the hope that Christmas brings, using them as a foundation for the year ahead.

The True Gift of Christmas

The true gift of Christmas is not found in the elaborate decorations, the grand feasts, or the expensive presents wrapped under the tree. While these elements certainly bring joy and festivity, they are not the essence of the holiday. The true gift of Christmas is far simpler and far more profound—it lies in the love we share with others, the kindness we offer, and the connections we nurture. It is found in the moments of togetherness, in the spirit of giving, and in the opportunity to reflect on the blessings that life offers. Christmas, at its heart, is a celebration of the intangible gifts that cannot be measured or bought, but that carry the most lasting and meaningful impact.

The love that we give to others is the most precious gift of all. Christmas is a time when we are reminded of the importance of showing love—whether to family, friends, or even strangers. The act of giving love is often expressed in many forms: a heartfelt card, a warm hug, a listening ear, or a simple word of encouragement. These gestures, while small in size, carry immense significance. The joy of Christmas comes not from receiving but from offering our love to others, without expectation or condition. It is in these moments of selfless giving that we discover the true spirit of the season—the power of human connection and the warmth that love brings into our lives. This Christmas, the true gift is not wrapped in glittering paper, but in the hearts we touch and the love we share.

Another aspect of the true gift of Christmas is the joy of giving. It's easy to get caught up in the pressure of buying expensive gifts or finding the perfect item, but Christmas reminds us that giving is not about the price tag or the material value. The true spirit of giving lies in the thought, care, and effort that goes into a gift. Whether it's a handmade ornament, a thoughtfully written note, or an act of service, these gifts carry far more meaning than anything that can be bought. Giving, when done with love and sincerity, becomes an expression of our hearts. The joy of giving isn't just about the act of providing something for another person; it's about the connection it creates, the emotions it stirs, and the memories it leaves behind. The true gift of Christmas is found in our willingness to give from the heart, to extend ourselves for others, and to create moments of joy and kindness that last well beyond the holiday season.

Perhaps one of the most powerful gifts of Christmas is the opportunity for reflection and renewal. Amid the festivities and celebrations, Christmas offers a time to pause and reflect on the year that has passed. It is a chance to express gratitude for the blessings we have received and to acknowledge the challenges we have overcome. This season invites us to reconnect with what truly matters—to appreciate our loved ones, to reflect on our growth, and to embrace the hope of a new beginning. The gift of Christmas, in this sense, is one of introspection and renewal. It offers us a moment to reset, to forgive past grievances, and to approach the coming year with renewed hope and a deeper sense of purpose.

Christmas is also a time for creating memories that last a lifetime. The true gift of Christmas is often not the tangible presents we give and receive, but the moments spent with those we love. It's the laughter shared around the dinner table, the quiet moments spent together by the fire, the songs sung together, and the stories passed down from one generation to the next. These moments create the true wealth of the holiday season—the memories that we will carry with us long after the decorations are packed away. In these shared experiences, we find the true spirit of Christmas: a celebration of family, friendship, and the joy of simply being present with those who matter most.

The true gift of Christmas is a reminder that the most meaningful things in life are often the simplest. It is in love, kindness, giving, gratitude, and the moments we share with others that we find the heart of Christmas. These gifts, while intangible, leave an impact that lasts far longer than anything material. As we move through this holiday season, let us focus not on the things we can buy or acquire, but on the gifts of the heart—the true gifts that make Christmas the meaningful and transformative season it is.

A Future Filled with Hope

As the year comes to a close and the holiday season unfolds, there's an undeniable sense of anticipation in the air—an eagerness for what lies ahead. Christmas, with its themes of hope, renewal, and new beginnings, naturally becomes a time to look forward to the future with optimism. The season carries with it a sense of possibility, a reminder that no matter the struggles or challenges we face, the dawn of a new year brings the promise of fresh opportunities and brighter days. The future, much like the spirit of Christmas, is full of hope—a hope that inspires us to move forward, to strive for better, and to embrace the unknown with courage and faith.

The future is often seen as a blank slate, waiting to be shaped by our choices, actions, and dreams. Christmas, in its essence, is a celebration of the potential that each new day brings. It is a reminder that, even in the darkest times, there is always hope for a better tomorrow. The story of Christmas itself—the birth of a child who brought love, peace, and hope into the world—is a powerful symbol of renewal and transformation. It reminds us that even the smallest spark of hope can ignite change, and that the future holds within it the potential for great things. The holiday season encourages us to hold onto that hope, to trust that better days are ahead, and to take the steps necessary to make those dreams a reality.

A future filled with hope is one that embraces the lessons learned from the past. Christmas often brings with it moments of reflection, a time to acknowledge the struggles we've faced and the growth we've achieved. It's a time to understand that challenges are not obstacles but stepping stones to personal growth and wisdom. As we reflect on the past year, we can see how each difficulty has shaped us, preparing us for the next chapter in our journey. Hope is not about ignoring the difficulties of life, but about understanding that they are part of the greater story—a story that unfolds in beautiful, unexpected ways. With each lesson learned, we build resilience, and with each setback, we gain strength. The future, then, becomes not something to fear, but something to embrace with a heart full of gratitude for all that we've learned.

The future is also about the dreams we nurture and the goals we set. Christmas encourages us to dream big and to believe that anything is possible. It reminds us that hope is not just a passive feeling but an active force—one that propels us forward, helping us to envision and work toward the life we want to create. It's about setting intentions, about looking ahead with a sense of purpose and passion, and about taking action to make those dreams come true. Whether it's a personal goal, a career aspiration, or a dream to make a difference in the world, the future is filled with the promise of possibility. Christmas invites us to envision the future we want and to take the first steps toward making that vision a reality.

Perhaps the most beautiful aspect of a future filled with hope is the sense of community and connection it brings. Christmas is a time for family, for friends, and for coming together to celebrate the good in our lives. Hope is not something we hold onto alone—it's something that is shared, nurtured, and grown within the relationships we cultivate. As we look to the future, it's important to remember that we are not walking this journey alone. We are supported by the people around us, by the love and care of those who walk beside us. The future, then, is not just about individual dreams but about collective hope—the hope that, together, we can build a better world, one filled with compassion, kindness, and unity.

A future filled with hope is not about waiting for change to happen; it is about creating it. It's about choosing to see the world through a lens of optimism, about embracing the opportunities that come our way, and about believing that the best is yet to come. Christmas reminds us of this power of hope—the ability to transform, to grow, and to create a future that is filled with possibility. As we celebrate the season, let us hold onto that hope, knowing that the future, with all its challenges and triumphs, is a gift waiting to be embraced with open arms. The future is not just a place we are heading; it is a canvas on which we can paint our dreams, a promise of all that is yet to come.

Chapter 9
The Whisper of Christmas Magic

There is an undeniable magic that fills the air during the Christmas season—a whisper that beckons to us from the quiet moments of reflection, from the twinkling lights on the tree, and from the laughter shared among loved ones. Christmas has a way of infusing everything with a sense of wonder, a feeling that the world is just a little bit more magical than usual. This magic is subtle, often unspoken, but deeply felt. It's a quiet sense of joy and peace that seems to settle over us, inviting us to believe in something greater than ourselves—a feeling of unity, love, and possibility that permeates the season.

The magic of Christmas isn't found in the material gifts we give or receive, nor is it in the perfectly wrapped presents or elaborate decorations. Instead, it is in the moments of togetherness, in the shared experiences that create lasting memories, and in the quiet moments of connection. Christmas has a way of slowing us down, encouraging us to look at the world through the eyes of wonder, as if everything—the snow, the music, the simple acts of kindness—is a reminder that magic exists in the everyday. It's a time when even the simplest things, like a warm drink by the fire or a heartfelt conversation, take on a deeper meaning, filled with the essence of the season.

The whisper of Christmas magic calls us to believe in the beauty of the season, to remember that there is joy in the little things, and to embrace the spirit of generosity and goodwill. It's a call to look beyond the material and embrace the intangible gifts of love, connection, and hope. This chapter will explore the quiet yet powerful magic that Christmas brings—how it transforms the ordinary into the extraordinary and fills our hearts with a sense of wonder, reminding us that the true essence of the season lies not in what we see, but in what we feel.

The Return of Old Traditions

In an era where modernity often sweeps us away with its fast-paced, ever-changing nature, there is something deeply comforting about the return of old traditions. Christmas, in particular, serves as a reminder of the timeless beauty that lies in the customs and practices passed down through generations. These traditions, some of which may have been neglected or altered over the years, bring with them a sense of continuity, a connection to the past, and an understanding that the essence of the holiday has always been rooted in love, family, and shared experiences. The return of these old traditions not only enriches our celebrations but also allows us to rediscover the magic of the season in its purest form.

The beauty of old Christmas traditions is that they often go beyond the material aspects of the holiday. While decorations, presents, and elaborate meals are certainly part of the Christmas experience, the traditions that endure through time carry with them deeper meanings. They are rituals that ground us in the season, that reconnect us to our heritage, and that serve as reminders of the values that make Christmas so meaningful. Whether it's the act of decorating the tree together as a family, baking holiday cookies using recipes passed down from grandparents, or attending a midnight service, these traditions are more than just customs—they are the heart and soul of Christmas itself.

One of the most beautiful things about rediscovering old traditions is that they allow us to reflect on the passage of time. As families grow and change, certain traditions may fall by the wayside, but when they are brought back into the fold, they create an opportunity to reflect on the moments of the past. These familiar customs carry memories with them—of loved ones who may no longer be present, of childhood moments that once felt so distant, and of the times when the world seemed simpler. When we revive these traditions, we not only honor the past but also ensure that it continues to shape our present and future. Each time we decorate the tree, prepare a favorite holiday dish, or sing the same carols, we are weaving a tapestry of memories that ties us to the generations before us, offering a sense of continuity and belonging.

The return of old traditions can also serve to anchor us in a world that often feels uncertain. In a society that is constantly evolving, traditions provide a sense of stability—a constant amidst the chaos. These familiar practices offer comfort in their predictability, giving us something to look forward to each year. The lighting of candles, the sharing of a special meal, or the reading of a beloved holiday story brings us back to a place of peace and tranquility. These rituals, often small and simple, provide a moment of pause, allowing us to step away from the noise of the world and reconnect with what truly matters. In reviving these traditions, we are not only honoring the past but also reaffirming the values that Christmas represents—love, generosity, family, and hope.

Reviving old Christmas traditions also has the power to bring families and communities closer together. It is in the shared experiences of preparing meals, wrapping gifts, or participating in a holiday service that we deepen our relationships. These traditions create moments of connection—moments that transcend generations and bring people together in ways that are meaningful and lasting. The return of these customs provides a sense of unity and belonging, as families gather around familiar rituals that reinforce their shared identity. These experiences are not just about the traditions themselves but about the bonds that are strengthened and the memories that are created as we partake in them together.

The return of old traditions serves as a gentle reminder that, while the world may change, the things that truly matter remain timeless. Christmas is not just about the gifts or the grand celebrations; it is about the love we share, the connections we nurture, and the values that we pass down to future generations. By reviving the old traditions that have been handed down through the years, we ensure that the spirit of Christmas remains alive and vibrant, filling our hearts with joy and gratitude for the past, the present, and the future. In embracing these timeless customs, we find that the true meaning of Christmas is not something that can be found in a store or wrapped in a box, but something that lives within us and is passed on through the generations.

A Christmas Wish Come True

Christmas is a time of magic, and for many, it's a season filled with hopes and wishes, both big and small. Whether it's the excitement of children writing letters to Santa Claus or the quiet wishes that adults hold close to their hearts, Christmas has a unique way of turning these dreams into reality, or at the very least, bringing them closer. The magic of the season is rooted not just in the presents we unwrap, but in the belief that anything is possible—that a wish, no matter how improbable, could come true. A Christmas wish come true is more than just a fairy tale; it's a moment of wonder and joy, a manifestation of the season's spirit of generosity, love, and goodwill.

At the heart of a Christmas wish is the hope for something greater—a desire for connection, peace, or fulfillment that transcends the material aspects of the holiday. Often, these wishes are not just for tangible gifts, but for emotional or spiritual fulfillment. A family might wish for reconciliation, a person may wish for good health, or a child might hope for a toy they've long dreamed about. It is in these simple, heartfelt wishes that the true magic of Christmas is found. Christmas is a time when these wishes, whether spoken or unspoken, are given special attention, when the world seems to slow down just enough to give us hope that our dreams, no matter how small or large, can come true.

A Christmas wish come true is often the result of love and thoughtfulness. In the season of giving, when we share not just material gifts but also our time, our energy, and our hearts, we see that some wishes are fulfilled not by magic but by the kindness and care of others. It could be a surprise gift from a friend who remembers something special you mentioned, or a moment of kindness from a stranger that reminds you of the goodness still present in the world. The essence of Christmas lies in these moments—when we witness the fulfillment of someone's wish because we've taken the time to listen, to care, and to act with love. The true gift of Christmas is not necessarily the physical object received, but the feeling that someone's wish has been honored and that love is at the core of it all.

Sometimes, a Christmas wish come true can be as simple as the joy of being together. For those who may be separated from family, friends, or loved ones during the holidays, the ultimate wish is often the return of these connections. Reuniting with family members after a long absence, spending time with someone who has been ill or far away, or simply sharing a peaceful moment with those we love—these are the moments that bring the true magic of Christmas to life. The wish to be surrounded by love, warmth, and togetherness can often be fulfilled in ways that don't require grand gestures but the quiet, everyday acts of love and presence that make the holiday season so special.

A Christmas wish come true is also a reminder of the power of hope and belief. As we grow older, it's easy to lose sight of the dreams and wishes we once held so tightly to. The magic of Christmas brings us back to that childlike belief in the impossible—that miracles can happen and that wishes, no matter how small, can be fulfilled. It teaches us that no matter how difficult life can be, there is always room for hope, for change, and for the possibility of a brighter future. Whether the wish is for personal success, the resolution of a long-standing challenge, or simply the peace of mind that comes from knowing we are loved, Christmas reminds us that we are never alone in our dreams.

Ultimately, the magic of a Christmas wish come true is not just about receiving what we wish for, but about the spirit of giving, love, and connection that makes the holiday season so meaningful. It's about the joy that comes from seeing someone else's wish fulfilled, the warmth that fills our hearts when we can make a difference in another person's life, and the belief that, with hope and love, anything is possible. Christmas is a time for wishes to come true—whether through small acts of kindness, cherished moments of togetherness, or the simple yet profound feeling that, at least for this season, the world is a little bit kinder, a little bit warmer, and a little bit more magical.

Forever in Our Hearts

At Christmas, we often find ourselves reflecting on the people who have touched our lives in profound ways—those who have been with us for many years, and those who have left us too soon. The holiday season, with its themes of love, family, and togetherness, brings both joy and sorrow as we remember those who are no longer physically present but whose spirits remain alive in our hearts. While the absence of loved ones can be felt more acutely during the holidays, it is in these moments of reflection that we realize how deeply their influence continues to shape our lives. Christmas, with its enduring message of hope and love, offers a special opportunity to honor and celebrate the memory of those who are forever in our hearts.

The holidays have a way of making us more aware of the people who have shaped our lives. Whether it's the traditions they started, the lessons they imparted, or the love they shared, their presence continues to resonate even in their absence. The quiet moments of Christmas, when we gather around the tree, share meals, or reflect on the year gone by, can often bring memories flooding back. It might be the scent of a favorite holiday dish that reminds us of a mother or grandmother, or the sound of a certain song that brings back fond memories of a lost friend. These moments of remembrance are powerful reminders that the people we love are never truly gone—they live on in the ways we continue to honor them, in the traditions we carry forward, and in the love we pass down to others.

Christmas is also a time when we celebrate the legacy of our loved ones. The stories we share, the rituals we uphold, and the love we give are all part of the inheritance they have left us. Even though they are no longer with us, they remain a part of our lives in the most meaningful ways. The ornaments on the Christmas tree, perhaps hand-crafted by a loved one who has passed, become symbols of their love and presence. A favorite holiday recipe, passed down through generations, keeps their spirit alive in every bite. These simple traditions remind us that their influence remains with us, guiding us through the seasons and shaping how we celebrate, love, and live. It is through these acts of remembrance that we honor those who have left us, ensuring that they are forever part of our holiday season and our hearts.

The loss of a loved one, especially during the holidays, can bring a sense of melancholy, yet it also offers an opportunity to reflect on the depth of love that transcends physical presence. The true meaning of Christmas is not bound by the decorations, the gifts, or the festivities; it is rooted in love. Love doesn't end with the passing of time or the end of life; it endures in our hearts, in the memories we cherish, and in the way we continue to honor the people who meant so much to us. This Christmas, as we gather with those who are still here, we can also take a moment to remember those who have gone before us, holding them close in our thoughts, in our prayers, and in the quiet, loving spaces of our hearts.

Though the pain of loss can never be fully erased, Christmas offers a chance for healing. The light of the season, the joy of giving, and the warmth of family and friends serve as reminders that love is eternal. As we reflect on those who are forever in our hearts, we find comfort in knowing that the love we share, the memories we hold, and the legacy we continue to carry forward are powerful forces that keep them close to us. Christmas is a time of new beginnings, and in remembering and honoring those we've lost, we find that they are never truly gone. They are forever a part of us—alive in our hearts, in our traditions, and in the ways we choose to love and live.

This Christmas, let us hold in our hearts not only those who are with us but also those who have gone before us. Let their memory be a beacon of love and hope, lighting our way through the holiday season and beyond. Though they may no longer be physically present, they remain forever in our hearts, guiding us with the love they gave, and the memories they left behind.

Chapter 10
The Spirit of Giving

The Christmas season is synonymous with the spirit of giving, a time when hearts are opened, and generosity flows freely. It's a season where we reflect on the true meaning of giving—not just in material gifts, but in sharing love, kindness, and our time with others. The act of giving during Christmas goes beyond the exchange of presents; it's about deepening connections, offering comfort, and spreading joy to those around us. This chapter explores the deeper essence of giving, examining how Christmas encourages us to embrace selflessness and generosity in all forms, enriching both the giver and the receiver.

The spirit of giving is not measured by the cost of gifts or the grandeur of gestures, but by the thoughtfulness and care that accompany them. Christmas teaches us that the most meaningful gifts are often the ones that come from the heart—small acts of kindness, a thoughtful gesture, or a shared moment of joy. It's a time to give not only material things but to offer our presence, our attention, and our love. By focusing on the quality and sincerity of what we give, Christmas inspires us to look beyond the material world and connect with others in more meaningful ways, deepening our relationships and fostering a sense of community.

Moreover, the spirit of giving at Christmas encourages us to expand our generosity beyond our immediate circles. While family and friends are the natural focus of our giving, Christmas is also a time to think of those less fortunate or those who may be struggling. It's a season when we are reminded to share our blessings with others—

whether through charitable acts, donations, or simply offering kindness to strangers. By embracing the broader spirit of giving, Christmas not only nurtures the bonds we have with our loved ones but also allows us to contribute to making the world a kinder, more compassionate place.

The True Meaning of Giving

At Christmas, the act of giving is central to the celebration. It's a time when we reflect on the spirit of generosity, the joy of sharing, and the significance of offering something meaningful to others. However, the true meaning of giving goes far beyond the exchange of material gifts. While giving presents is a beloved tradition, the essence of giving during Christmas—and in life—is rooted in love, thoughtfulness, and connection. True giving is not measured by the cost of a gift or the size of a gesture, but by the intent behind it and the positive impact it has on the recipient and the giver.

At its core, the true meaning of giving is about showing care and appreciation for others. It's about taking the time to think of what might bring joy or comfort to someone else, and then offering that gift with a full heart. Whether it's a beautifully wrapped present or a simple handwritten card, the value of a gift lies in the thought, effort, and love behind it. This type of giving transcends material possessions—it's about expressing kindness, creating memories, and deepening relationships. When we give from the heart, our actions communicate that the recipient matters, that their well-being is important to us, and that we're willing to invest time and energy in making their life a little brighter.

True giving also goes beyond material gifts to encompass the giving of time, attention, and emotional support. Sometimes, the most valuable gift we can offer someone is our presence. In a world that moves so fast, offering a moment to listen, a hand to hold, or a moment of genuine connection can mean more than any physical object. Acts of service, such as preparing a meal for a friend, visiting someone who is lonely, or offering a helping hand during a difficult time, can be among the most meaningful gifts of all. These acts of kindness reflect a deeper kind of giving—a giving that is focused on nurturing relationships and creating a sense of community. Christmas reminds us that the greatest gifts are not always the ones we can hold in our hands, but those we give through our hearts and actions.

The true meaning of giving also extends to selflessness—giving without expecting anything in return. Christmas is a season that encourages us to embrace this aspect of giving. Whether we are giving a gift, our time, or our love, the spirit of Christmas teaches us to give freely, without strings attached, without any anticipation of rewards. It's about offering something of ourselves purely for the joy of making someone else's life a little better. This selflessness is at the heart of Christmas—the way we embrace the holiday is through acts of kindness, love, and generosity that reflect the giving nature of the season. When we give in this way, we enrich our own lives as well, experiencing the joy that comes from seeing others happy, knowing we've made a difference.

Furthermore, true giving involves empathy. It is about understanding the needs of others, whether they are physical, emotional, or spiritual. Christmas calls us to look outside of ourselves and consider how we can meet the needs of others in meaningful ways. This could mean supporting those who are less fortunate, volunteering time, or simply being there for someone who may be struggling. The holiday season, with its emphasis on love and goodwill, reminds us that true giving is rooted in compassion and a desire to help others, not just during the festive season, but throughout the year.

Ultimately, the true meaning of giving during Christmas is not about the material gifts we exchange but about fostering a spirit of generosity, kindness, and connection. It is about offering our love, time, and resources to others, enriching their lives and deepening the bonds that connect us all. Through this giving, we embody the spirit of Christmas—love, compassion, and hope—and create a world that is brighter, more compassionate, and full of joy. Giving from the heart, with selflessness and empathy, is the most enduring gift we can offer and the true essence of what makes Christmas so special.

The Joy of Giving from the Heart

There is an unparalleled joy in giving from the heart, a deep sense of fulfillment that transcends the material aspects of the holiday season. At Christmas, the act of giving becomes a powerful reminder that the true spirit of the season is rooted in love, kindness, and connection. While gifts wrapped in beautiful paper and adorned with ribbons are an important part of the festivities, it's the thought, intention, and love behind the giving that makes it truly meaningful. When we give from the heart, we offer not just a physical gift, but a piece of ourselves—our time, attention, care, and genuine affection. This type of giving creates lasting connections and leaves an impact far beyond the holiday season.

Giving from the heart begins with a deep understanding of the other person's needs, desires, and circumstances. It's not about spending large amounts of money or finding the most extravagant gift; rather, it's about offering something that reflects the recipient's interests or needs. When we give from the heart, we take the time to consider what will bring joy, comfort, or meaning to the other person's life. A carefully chosen gift, a handwritten letter, or an act of service that shows thoughtfulness and empathy are often the most cherished. This kind of giving comes with the knowledge that what we offer carries the weight of our affection and care, making it far more valuable than any material object.

One of the most beautiful aspects of giving from the heart is that it creates a sense of connection between the giver and the receiver. When we give with genuine intent, we're not simply exchanging objects; we are deepening relationships, expressing appreciation, and fostering bonds that are based on mutual love and respect. The joy of giving is found not in the act itself but in the emotional connection it nurtures. It is about showing someone that they are valued, loved, and cared for, whether it's through a thoughtful gesture, a surprise visit, or simply spending time with them. This shared experience of giving creates lasting memories and fosters a sense of unity that goes far beyond the holiday season.

Moreover, the joy of giving from the heart is not only experienced by the recipient but also by the giver. There is a special kind of joy that comes from selflessly giving to others—one that enriches the spirit and fills the heart with warmth. When we give with love, without expectation of anything in return, we experience a sense of fulfillment that is hard to describe. This is the kind of joy that comes from knowing we have made a positive impact in someone else's life, from knowing that our actions have brought happiness, comfort, or peace to another person. Giving from the heart is not just about the recipient—it also brings a sense of deep satisfaction to the giver, enriching their own life in the process.

Additionally, giving from the heart reminds us of the importance of love, compassion, and generosity in our everyday lives. Christmas provides a perfect backdrop for this kind of giving, but it's not limited to the holiday season. The joy that comes from giving with sincerity is something we can carry with us throughout the year. Whether it's a simple compliment, offering our time to help others, or sharing a kind word with someone in need, these everyday acts of kindness reflect the true essence of giving. When we give from the heart, we embody the spirit of love and generosity that Christmas represents and carry it into every corner of our lives.

In essence, the joy of giving from the heart is one of the most fulfilling and enriching experiences we can have. It is about offering something meaningful, not because it is expected or because of any personal gain, but because we genuinely care for others and want to bring joy into their lives. This kind of giving creates connections, fosters compassion, and spreads love in ways that are lasting and deeply impactful. The true joy of giving is found in the act itself—the thoughtfulness, the love, and the heartfelt intention behind it. This Christmas, and beyond, let us embrace the joy of giving from the heart, knowing that the love and care we share will continue to resonate long after the holiday season ends.

Giving Beyond Material Gifts

While the holiday season is often associated with the exchange of material gifts, the true essence of giving transcends the physical items we unwrap and place under the tree. Christmas, in its purest form, is about much more than the gifts we give or receive. It's about offering something more meaningful—gifts of love, kindness, time, and connection. The act of giving beyond material gifts is a reminder that the most valuable presents are often intangible and cannot be bought or wrapped in a box. These types of gifts come from the heart and leave a lasting impact that far outlasts any material possession.

One of the most profound ways to give beyond material gifts is by offering our time and attention to others. In a world that moves at a fast pace, where everyone is busy with their own lives, the gift of time can be one of the most precious things we can offer. Taking time to truly listen, to be present with someone, or to spend quality time together can make all the difference. Whether it's visiting a friend who's feeling lonely, helping a neighbor with a task, or simply sitting down for a conversation, the gift of your time shows others that they matter. This kind of giving doesn't require any special preparation or cost; it simply requires a willingness to be present and a desire to make a meaningful connection. These moments of togetherness, shared laughter, and support are often remembered far longer than any material gift.

Another form of giving beyond material gifts is the gift of kindness and compassion. During Christmas, we are reminded of the importance of showing love and empathy to others, especially those who may be going through difficult times. Offering a kind word, extending a helping hand, or offering support in times of need are all gifts that can have a profound impact. Christmas provides the perfect opportunity to give back to the community—whether it's through volunteering at a food bank, donating clothes to those in need, or simply reaching out to someone who is struggling. These acts of kindness create a ripple effect, spreading love and warmth throughout our communities. The beauty of these gifts is that they are not limited by wealth or resources; anyone, regardless of their circumstances, can offer kindness and make a difference in someone's life.

The gift of forgiveness is perhaps one of the most powerful ways to give beyond material gifts. At Christmas, when emotions can run high, old wounds and misunderstandings can resurface. However, Christmas offers us an opportunity to let go of grudges, to forgive past hurts, and to heal relationships. The act of forgiveness doesn't just release others from their mistakes—it also frees us from the burden of resentment. By choosing to forgive, we give the gift of peace, not only to the other person but to ourselves as well. This gift of emotional healing strengthens relationships, restores trust, and fosters a sense of unity that is at the heart of the Christmas spirit. It is a gift that requires no wrapping, no price tag, but offers immeasurable value in the restoration of love and connection.

Lastly, giving beyond material gifts involves sharing knowledge and wisdom. Christmas can be a time of reflection and learning, a moment to pass on valuable life lessons, insights, or stories to others. Whether it's offering advice, mentoring someone, or sharing a piece of wisdom that has helped you in your life, these gifts can have a lasting impact on others' lives. The gift of knowledge not only empowers the recipient but also creates a bond of trust and mutual respect. It is a gift that grows with time, helping others to navigate their challenges and reach their potential.

In conclusion, giving beyond material gifts is a reminder that the most meaningful gifts in life are those that come from the heart. Whether through the gift of time, kindness, forgiveness, or wisdom, these acts of giving create lasting memories and strengthen the connections we share with others. Christmas teaches us that the value of a gift lies not in its price but in its ability to enrich someone's life, foster love and compassion, and create bonds that endure. In a world focused on material possessions, it is the intangible gifts—the ones that come from within—that truly define the spirit of Christmas and bring the most joy to both the giver and the receiver.

Chapter 11

A Christmas of Peace

Christmas is often seen as a time of celebration, joy, and giving, but at its core, the holiday also carries a powerful message of peace. In a world that is sometimes filled with division, conflict, and stress, Christmas offers a moment of respite, a chance to come together in harmony and reflect on the greater ideals of love and goodwill. It is a season that calls us to pause, to find common ground, and to embrace the peace that can be found within ourselves and in our relationships. This chapter explores the theme of peace during Christmas, a peace that is both personal and collective, and the ways in which the spirit of the season fosters healing, reconciliation, and unity.

The peace that Christmas embodies is not just the absence of conflict, but the presence of compassion, understanding, and kindness. It's about extending goodwill to others, even those with whom we may have disagreements, and creating a space where love can flourish. During the holiday season, we are encouraged to put aside past grievances, to forgive, and to approach our relationships with a renewed sense of empathy. Christmas reminds us that true peace is not just about creating calm on the surface, but about fostering deep connections based on mutual respect and care. It is in these moments of peace that the true essence of the holiday is felt — the warmth of family, the joy of togetherness, and the comfort of knowing that we are all united by the bonds of love.

Finally, a Christmas of peace encourages us to look beyond our immediate circles and consider the broader world. The message of

Christmas calls us to embrace peace on a global scale, to contribute to creating a world where understanding, kindness, and unity are the guiding principles. Whether through acts of charity, support for those in need, or standing up for justice, Christmas provides an opportunity to reflect on how we can contribute to building a more peaceful world. As we share the peace of Christmas within our homes and communities, we are reminded that this peace is not just for the season, but for every day, inspiring us to work together toward a world filled with love and compassion.

The Call for Unity

Christmas, a time of love, joy, and reflection, carries with it a powerful call for unity—an invitation to come together, set aside differences, and embrace the shared values that bind us as human beings. In a world that is often divided by conflict, misunderstandings, and struggles, Christmas offers a moment to pause and reflect on the strength that comes from unity. The message of Christmas urges us to recognize that, despite our varied backgrounds, beliefs, and experiences, we all share the fundamental need for love, compassion, and connection. The spirit of Christmas calls us to embrace these universal truths, fostering a sense of unity that transcends the superficial divisions that too often separate us.

At the heart of Christmas is the idea of togetherness—of family, friends, and communities coming together to celebrate the season, share meals, and create memories. This collective experience reminds us that we are stronger when we unite. The Christmas table, the holiday traditions, and the shared moments of joy all serve as symbols of this unity. They encourage us to focus not on our differences but on the common bonds we share as human beings. Christmas invites us to let go of pride, resentment, and divisiveness, and instead embrace the love and understanding that can only come when we make the conscious decision to come together as one.

Whether it's through a simple act of kindness, a heartfelt conversation, or a shared experience, these moments of togetherness create the foundation for a more compassionate and harmonious world.

The call for unity at Christmas is not limited to our immediate circles. It extends to the world around us, encouraging us to look beyond our own families and communities and to consider how we can contribute to the larger global family. Christmas offers a unique opportunity to reflect on our role in fostering peace and understanding on a wider scale. This is a time when we are called to step outside of ourselves and consider the challenges faced by others—whether they are individuals in our communities or people across the globe facing poverty, injustice, or hardship. Through acts of charity, support for social causes, or simply extending kindness to those around us, we have the power to spread the message of unity to the world. The message of Christmas reminds us that we are all connected, and by fostering unity on a global scale, we contribute to creating a more peaceful and just world.

Unity, however, is not just about coming together for the sake of celebration or charity; it is also about reconciliation and healing. Christmas provides an opportunity to forgive and rebuild relationships that may have been strained over time. In families, workplaces, and communities, conflicts can arise, and misunderstandings can build walls between us. Yet Christmas, with its emphasis on peace, love, and forgiveness, invites us to mend those fences. The act of forgiveness is a powerful force in bringing people together, allowing us to release past hurts and embrace the potential for renewed connection. Christmas encourages us to recognize that unity is not about agreeing on everything, but about understanding, respecting, and accepting one another despite our differences.

Ultimately, the call for unity during Christmas is a call for us to be our best selves—to look beyond our differences and to focus on what unites us as people. It's about fostering a sense of compassion, understanding, and empathy that transcends boundaries. It's about recognizing that in the grand scheme of life, the things that divide us are far smaller than the things that unite us. Christmas serves as a reminder of the strength that comes from unity—the way it can transform lives, communities, and the world. As we celebrate the season, let us heed the call for unity, embracing the love and connection that Christmas inspires and working together to create a world where peace, kindness, and understanding prevail.

Inner Peace Through Reflection

In the busyness of daily life, it is easy to become consumed by external demands—work, family obligations, societal expectations, and personal goals. These pressures can create a constant whirlwind of activity, leaving little room for stillness and introspection. Yet, one of the most powerful ways to achieve inner peace is through reflection—a practice that invites us to slow down, connect with ourselves, and find clarity in the midst of chaos. Christmas, with its quieter moments and emphasis on introspection, offers the perfect opportunity to pause and engage in reflection. This season of peace encourages us to look inward, to assess our emotions, and to cultivate a sense of tranquility that comes from understanding and accepting who we are.

Inner peace through reflection begins with creating space for quiet. During the holiday season, when the external world can feel overwhelming with its celebrations, shopping, and festivities, it is crucial to carve out moments of stillness. It might be as simple as taking a quiet walk in nature, sitting by the fire with a cup of tea, or spending a few moments in solitude before the hustle of the day begins. In these moments of silence, we allow ourselves the time and space to listen—to listen to our thoughts, to the emotions we may be carrying, and to the deeper parts of ourselves that often go unnoticed. Reflection is an invitation to pause, breathe, and simply be with ourselves, without distractions or interruptions.

Through reflection, we gain the opportunity to examine the past year—its highs and lows, its successes and struggles—and understand how these experiences have shaped us. Christmas, with its emphasis on renewal, offers a natural point to look back, but also to look forward. What have we learned from our challenges? What moments have brought us joy, peace, or growth? This reflection is not about self-criticism but about self-awareness. It allows us to acknowledge our journey, honor the lessons we have learned, and release any negative emotions or patterns that may be holding us back. By accepting and embracing both the good and the difficult moments, we free ourselves to move forward with a lighter heart and a deeper sense of understanding.

Moreover, inner peace through reflection also involves forgiveness. Christmas often brings families and friends together, and with this proximity can come unresolved conflicts or old wounds. Reflection offers us the opportunity to examine these relationships and consider whether we are holding onto any grudges or resentment. True inner peace cannot exist if we are carrying emotional baggage. Christmas invites us to forgive—not just others, but ourselves. Forgiving others for past hurt and forgiving ourselves for mistakes made allows us to release the emotional weight that keeps us from experiencing peace. The act of forgiveness is not about excusing wrongs but about liberating ourselves from the toxic energy that resentment creates. It's an essential part of the reflection process, as it clears the way for healing and growth.

Reflection also helps us clarify our intentions and priorities for the year ahead. The quiet introspection that Christmas inspires allows us to reconnect with what truly matters to us. In a world that often emphasizes external achievement, we may lose sight of our own inner desires and values. Through reflection, we can realign ourselves with our core beliefs and set intentions that are in harmony with our authentic self. This self-awareness creates a sense of peace because it allows us to act in alignment with our values, rather than being swayed by external pressures. When we know what we truly want and why, we can approach the future with clarity and confidence, knowing that we are living in accordance with our true self.

Ultimately, inner peace through reflection is about creating balance in our lives. It's a process of turning inward, examining our thoughts and feelings, and giving ourselves permission to slow down and be present. Christmas, with its quiet beauty and message of renewal, is the perfect time to practice reflection. It allows us to find peace not in the external world but in the quiet space within. In these moments of stillness, we reconnect with ourselves, heal old wounds, and set new intentions, all of which lead to a deeper sense of inner peace that can carry us through the year ahead. Reflection is a gift we give ourselves—a chance to rest, to understand, and to find peace amidst the noise of the world.

The Legacy of Peace Beyond Christmas

Christmas is a season of peace, but its true power lies in its ability to inspire lasting change, extending the spirit of peace far beyond the holiday itself. The traditions, values, and messages of Christmas, while profoundly felt during the season, are meant to ripple through the year, influencing the way we interact with others and the world around us. The legacy of peace beyond Christmas is about more than just a temporary feeling of goodwill—it is about cultivating a lasting peace within ourselves and spreading that peace outward into our relationships, communities, and the broader world. Christmas offers the opportunity to reflect on what true peace means and how we can carry that sense of harmony forward throughout the year.

The peace of Christmas often begins with personal reflection. During the holiday season, we are encouraged to pause, reflect on our lives, and reset our intentions. It is a time for introspection, for reconciling with ourselves and others, and for releasing negative emotions like resentment and anger. This internal peace—achieved through self-forgiveness, understanding, and gratitude—is the foundation for peace that extends outward. The legacy of peace beyond Christmas begins when we take the lessons learned during the holiday season and apply them to our daily lives. The act of maintaining inner peace is not a one-time event but a continuous practice that requires mindfulness, patience, and compassion.

When we cultivate inner peace, it naturally influences our interactions with others. The peace we experience during Christmas encourages us to extend kindness and understanding to those around us—whether it's family, friends, or even strangers. By carrying the spirit of Christmas forward, we become ambassadors of peace, seeking to foster harmony and goodwill in our relationships. This might involve forgiving someone we've had a long-standing disagreement with, offering a listening ear to someone in need, or simply approaching each interaction with kindness and empathy. The legacy of peace beyond Christmas is found in the small, everyday acts of love and respect that we offer to others. These gestures, though seemingly small, can have a profound impact, helping to create a more peaceful environment in our homes, workplaces, and communities.

Beyond our immediate circles, the legacy of peace can have a broader impact on the world. Christmas's message of peace and goodwill is not limited to the personal or familial sphere—it calls us to consider how we can contribute to peace on a global scale. Whether it's through charitable giving, advocating for justice, or standing up for those who are oppressed, the peace we celebrate at Christmas can inspire us to take action in support of a more just and peaceful world. Christmas reminds us that our individual efforts, no matter how small, can contribute to the larger goal of creating a world where peace, equality, and compassion are the guiding principles. The legacy of peace beyond Christmas challenges us to make this a reality, not just during the holiday season but every day.

This legacy is also nurtured by the spirit of community. Christmas emphasizes the importance of coming together, of creating spaces where people feel accepted, valued, and loved. As we carry this sense of community forward, we recognize the importance of building inclusive, supportive spaces in our society. The idea of community peace extends to our neighborhoods, our workplaces, and the global community. By fostering environments where people can express themselves freely, where differences are respected, and where everyone's voice is heard, we contribute to a lasting legacy of peace. This sense of belonging and unity is something that Christmas teaches us but must be continually cultivated year-round.

Finally, the legacy of peace beyond Christmas is about leaving a positive imprint on the world. Just as Christmas calls us to reflect on the impact of our actions, it also encourages us to leave behind a legacy that will outlast the season. This can be achieved through acts of kindness, creating meaningful relationships, and working toward a more compassionate and just world. The peace of Christmas is not just a temporary feeling; it is a force that, when carried into every facet of our lives, can transform the way we live and interact with the world. The legacy of peace is one that extends far beyond the holiday season, enriching the lives of those around us and creating a lasting ripple effect that promotes love, harmony, and understanding in the world.

In essence, the legacy of peace beyond Christmas is about embodying the values of the season every day. By nurturing inner peace, fostering kindness, and working toward a more peaceful world, we ensure that the spirit of Christmas continues to thrive long after the decorations are taken down. The true gift of Christmas is not just in the season itself, but in how we carry its message of peace with us, transforming our world and the world of those around us.

Chapter 12
The Gift of New Beginnings

As Christmas marks the end of another year, it naturally invites reflection on the past and anticipation for what the future holds. The holiday season, with its messages of hope, renewal, and new beginnings, offers a unique opportunity to let go of the past and embrace the future with optimism and intention. This chapter explores the profound gift of new beginnings that Christmas offers—not just as a fresh start on the calendar, but as an invitation to transform ourselves and our lives. Christmas reminds us that every ending is also a beginning, and in the quiet moments of the season, we can embrace the chance to create a new chapter in our journey.

New beginnings are not just about making resolutions or setting goals; they are about renewing our spirit and reconnecting with what truly matters. Christmas provides the perfect backdrop for this process, encouraging us to reflect on the lessons of the past year and to think about the changes we want to make moving forward. Whether it's a shift in mindset, a new project, or a change in personal habits, Christmas serves as a time of inner renewal—helping us understand that we have the power to create positive changes in our lives. The season teaches us that the gift of new beginnings is not just about what we do differently, but about how we approach life with a renewed sense of purpose and passion.

The gift of new beginnings is also a reminder that we are not defined by our past mistakes or setbacks. Christmas, with its message of forgiveness and second chances, encourages us to release any guilt, regret, or negativity we may carry. It reminds us that every new day is an opportunity to start fresh, to embrace hope, and to take steps toward becoming the person we aspire to be. This chapter explores how the spirit of Christmas encourages us to break free from the constraints of the past and move forward with renewed energy and an open heart, ready to embrace the possibilities that the future holds.

Letting Go of the Past

Letting go of the past is one of the most freeing and empowering acts we can undertake, especially as we approach a time of renewal, like Christmas and the New Year. Our memories, both joyful and painful, shape who we are, but they also have the potential to hold us back if we remain tethered to them too tightly. The act of letting go allows us to release old emotional burdens and make space for new possibilities, growth, and healing. Christmas, with its themes of forgiveness, new beginnings, and peace, provides the perfect opportunity to reflect on the past and embrace the future with a clear heart and mind.

The past, with all its triumphs and regrets, can become a source of emotional weight if we don't learn to let go. We often carry old wounds—unresolved conflicts, missed opportunities, or past mistakes—that shape our present decisions and relationships. These memories can be difficult to move past, as they often become part of our identity, influencing how we view ourselves and the world around us. However, Christmas offers us a chance to reflect on these experiences, understand their impact on our lives, and choose to release the grip they have over us. By acknowledging the lessons learned and accepting that we cannot change what has already happened, we free ourselves to move forward with a sense of peace. Letting go of the past doesn't mean forgetting it; it means choosing not to let it control our emotions or dictate our actions.

A crucial part of letting go is forgiveness—both of others and ourselves. Christmas teaches us the power of forgiveness, offering a chance to release feelings of resentment, anger, or guilt that we may have been holding onto. When we forgive, we let go of the emotional burden that comes with holding grudges or dwelling on past wrongs. Forgiveness allows us to free ourselves from the chains of bitterness and opens up the possibility for healing and reconciliation. This process is not always easy, especially if the pain runs deep. However, forgiveness is ultimately a gift we give ourselves, as it releases us from the emotional prison of the past. Christmas, with its message of peace and goodwill, offers us the perfect opportunity to reflect on who we need to forgive and begin the process of emotional release.

Letting go of the past also means releasing unrealistic expectations or attachments to what could have been. At times, we cling to the idea of how we wanted things to unfold, whether in relationships, careers, or life in general. When we're unable to accept things as they are, we become trapped in a cycle of disappointment, regret, or resentment. The Christmas season, with its focus on renewal, encourages us to release these attachments and accept the present moment. Instead of yearning for what we don't have, we can choose to focus on what we do have—embracing the beauty and opportunities that exist right in front of us. Letting go of expectations frees us to experience life as it is, with all its imperfections, joys, and challenges.

Finally, letting go of the past is an act of self-care and self-love. It's about recognizing that we deserve to move forward, to find happiness, and to embrace the future with an open heart. Christmas reminds us that we are deserving of peace and joy, and that we don't need to carry the weight of the past with us into the New Year. By letting go, we give ourselves the opportunity to heal, grow, and step into the new beginnings that await us. It's an invitation to let go of what no longer serves us and to make room for new experiences, relationships, and opportunities.

In conclusion, letting go of the past is not about forgetting or disregarding our experiences—it's about freeing ourselves from the emotional burden they carry. Christmas, with its message of forgiveness, renewal, and hope, offers us the perfect opportunity to reflect on the past, learn from it, and choose to release what holds us back. Letting go is a powerful act of self-liberation that allows us to embrace the present moment, heal old wounds, and step into the future with an open heart. By letting go, we make space for peace, growth, and the beautiful possibilities that await us.

Embracing Hope and Renewal

Christmas is a time of transformation, a season that invites us to embrace hope and renewal with open arms. It is a time when we look forward to new possibilities, new beginnings, and the chance to start afresh. At its core, Christmas offers the gift of hope—a belief that no matter how challenging the past year has been, there is always the potential for change, growth, and a brighter future. Embracing hope and renewal during this season is not just about setting resolutions for the year ahead but about reconnecting with the idea that each day holds the possibility for transformation. It is about letting go of past disappointments and embracing the future with optimism and faith.

Hope, at its essence, is the belief that good things are possible, even when the path ahead is uncertain. Christmas encourages us to reconnect with this sense of possibility. The story of Christmas itself—of new beginnings, of light coming into the world in a time of darkness—is a reminder that hope can be born in the most unexpected of places. Whether it's the birth of a child, the love shared with family and friends, or the kindness extended to those in need, Christmas highlights the beauty that exists in the world and reminds us that even small acts of love and kindness can create ripples of change. By embracing this hope, we remind ourselves that no matter where we are in life, there is always the potential for something better. Christmas teaches us that hope is not just a passive feeling but a powerful force that can guide us through adversity and inspire us to create a future filled with possibility.

In addition to hope, Christmas also brings the gift of renewal—a fresh start, a chance to leave behind the mistakes, regrets, and challenges of the past. The end of the year provides a natural opportunity for reflection, allowing us to take stock of what we have learned, how we have grown, and what we want to change in the future. Embracing renewal means acknowledging that we are not bound by our past, and that each new year offers the chance to reinvent ourselves. This renewal isn't about forgetting where we have come from, but about using those experiences as stepping stones to create the life we desire. Christmas invites us to let go of the burdens that weigh us down—whether they are emotional, mental, or physical—and embrace the freedom that comes with starting anew. In doing so, we open ourselves up to the opportunity to cultivate a life filled with purpose, joy, and fulfillment.

Embracing hope and renewal also involves cultivating a mindset of gratitude and positivity. By focusing on what we have rather than what we lack, we can create a sense of abundance that attracts more of the things we want in life. Christmas encourages us to appreciate the present moment and to recognize the blessings that already exist around us. This gratitude fuels our hope for the future, reminding us that we have the strength and resources to face whatever challenges come our way. Renewal, then, is not just about changing our external circumstances but about shifting our inner mindset. It's about choosing to see opportunities instead of obstacles, and to believe in our ability to create change, no matter how big or small.

Hope and renewal are also tied to the concept of healing. Christmas is a time when many people come together to heal old wounds—whether it's mending relationships, forgiving past grievances, or finding peace within ourselves. Embracing hope means believing in the possibility of healing and the power of forgiveness. It is a reminder that we can move forward, even after experiencing pain, loss, or heartache. The process of renewal is often one of emotional and spiritual healing, where we learn to release negative emotions, find closure, and open ourselves to new beginnings. This healing process, while personal, also connects us to the greater community, reminding us that we are not alone in our journey of transformation.

In conclusion, embracing hope and renewal during Christmas is about more than simply wishing for a better future—it is about taking actionable steps toward creating that future. By reconnecting with hope, we tap into a powerful force that inspires us to move forward, even when things feel uncertain. By embracing renewal, we give ourselves permission to start fresh, to heal, and to grow. Christmas, with its message of love, peace, and new beginnings, is the perfect time to embrace these gifts and to step into the new year with confidence, optimism, and a renewed sense of purpose. Through hope and renewal, we create a future that reflects the beauty of the season—a future filled with possibility, growth, and joy.

Conclusion

As we reach the end of our journey through Whispers of Christmas: A Tale of Joy and Wonder, we are reminded of the many layers that make Christmas a time of profound reflection, renewal, and connection. From the spirit of giving to the call for unity, from the joy of togetherness to the peace that resides within us, this season holds powerful lessons that extend far beyond the decorations, the gifts, and the traditions. Christmas invites us to slow down, to look inward, and to remember the true essence of what it means to live with love, compassion, and hope.

Through the stories shared in this book, we've explored the transformative power of Christmas—a season that encourages us to embrace the present, let go of the past, and open our hearts to the possibility of new beginnings. Whether it's the act of giving from the heart, the peaceful moments of reflection, or the chance to start anew, Christmas provides us with an opportunity to create lasting change in our lives and in the world around us. As we embrace the legacy of peace, we learn that true change begins within us— through forgiveness, through kindness, and through the decision to live with intention and purpose.

At its heart, Christmas is not simply about celebrating the birth of a child or enjoying festive traditions, but about embodying the values that make the world a kinder, more compassionate place. The gift of Christmas is not just in the material things we give or receive, but in the intangible qualities that remain long after the season has passed. Love, hope, unity, forgiveness, and joy—these are the gifts that carry forward, shaping our lives and the lives of those around us.

As we move through each season, it's easy to forget the lessons Christmas brings. Life can get busy, and the challenges of the world can sometimes dim our hope. However, Christmas reminds us that the true magic lies in our ability to carry these lessons with us. The essence of Christmas lives in every act of kindness, every moment of reflection, and every new beginning we embrace. It is a call to live with an open heart, to give freely without expecting anything in return, and to remember that every new day holds the possibility for peace, joy, and transformation.

In closing, Whispers of Christmas is an invitation to carry the spirit of the season into every moment of our lives. Whether we are in times of joy or challenge, we are reminded that the gifts we hold—the gift of hope, the gift of renewal, and the gift of love—are timeless treasures. Christmas does not end with the turning of the calendar; it continues to live within us, urging us to create a world filled with peace, compassion, and unity. The true magic of Christmas is not something we wait for, but something we choose to carry forward with us every day of the year. May we all embrace the true meaning of Christmas in our hearts, and may that joy and wonder inspire us to live with purpose, love, and peace, both now and in the years to come.

www.ingramcontent.com/pod-product-compliance
Lightning Source LLC
LaVergne TN
LVHW061040070526
838201LV00073B/5118